Young American Blues

Poetic Works
1984 - 2001

D.J. Haliday

Young American Blues,
Poetic Works 1984-2001

© 2011 by D.J. Haliday.

ISBN-978-0-9847218-0-1

Library of Congress
Cataloging in Publication Data

First Edition
Original Printing 2011

For information contact Poetry Attic Press at
www.poetryattic.com

Effervescent Ecstasy *(1984)*   *1*

Aloof Inside the Cockpit
Searching for the Promised Land *(1985)*   *97*

The Modern Mountain *(1986)*   *127*

Fleas Inside the Store *(1987)*   *159*

SouLfood to GoGo *(1988)*   *241*

Nature is Not for Cardboard Boxes *(1989)*   *311*

A Buskin for the Frump *(1995)*   *367*

GrUnGE *(1996)* 435

Spring Rain Independence *(2001)*

Effervescent Ecstasy

Melted Pennies

I kissed a star once
In a Northern blue sky
A small one perhaps
But it glowed in some eyes

This is for that little girl
Now ageless with the blues
One just pretends alone
Love's better felt in twos

Melted Pennies from Camelot
Buried deep beneath the rot
Of everyday verite'
There's ugliness in changing ways

Ho, wander -- What a blow!
Which direction did she go?
Through the cages or the clouds
Everybody had their doubts
Drinking Stouts
Drinking Stouts
Stumbling through and through
I tumble in my brew
How the midnight hassles dawn
How the boys all laugh at yawns
Prawns served deliciously
Til' someone cries *They cost too much!*
Wandering endlessly – crazy mind
Can't decide, when's the time
Nonsense better as a rule
Not locked up like a lonely fool

     Moonlight glowing
         Sad face calling
              What's worth knowing?

With the wind we fly
Like a bird we die
In the meantime what's the use
Of crying, trying
When all seems hopeless
Ropeless
Full of distress
Caught always undressed
What a mess!
In the morning if it comes
I'll still be living in the slums
A life of crumbs
I'd like I wish so many dreams
I sometimes lose my life it seems

Did the night once seem more precious?
A mystery divine?
A poem? A rhyme? A fruitful wine?
Endless temptation all the time?

Where is that beauty with the cool blue eyes?
The one I used to pump full of lies
I didn't mean it, I only tried
To be a lover in a wolf's disguise

Where has all the nonsense gone?
What then happened to Arthur's throne?
I've been to court and been conceded
Been received, deceived and grieved
Poor sad lonely king
I regret myself again
Grant me grace and inner peace
Leave me one I'll truly please
Released from tease, I'm appalled
Mattress stains from quite a bawl
But you little girl who's grown as I
Can you look into another's eye
And cry, honestly cry, honestly?
Would you die honestly for your lies?
Despise your every unjust whim?
Every show?

I knew you troubadour
I knew two troubadours
And we all might sin the same
Point our fingers at those insane
But where's the rain?
Pain
Where's the rain that washes the pain?
Stain
Left on the unwashed windowpane
What is your name?
Can you claim to be all right
In the dead of night
Sleeping or alone in fright
The night
Built in pain and eased with pleasure
How do you measure?
Why do scold?
What's the treasure that you behold?

Twas you I once adored
You thought I knew no common sense
But I was truly bored
With everything but you and I
Then I couldn't see

Snowstorms are wicked
Cold like the sea
In frigid death I've contemplated
All that you once meant to me
I thought it best to burn the verse
Romantic dreams are a silly curse
Sober a hearse
It's all for the worse
Scribble monkeys scratch your tongues
Yell what's pleasurable with your lungs
Hobble Hooble Heeble Wah
Hundle Hoodle Hoddle Bah!
Sunshine's hard to swallow
Sitting in the desert
Hearts are kind of hollow
When used as last resort

And I'm weary
Sometimes dead tired
But at this young confounded age
Full of spark and hot with fire
Retire? No!
I'll never slow
Think of what I long to know
I'm amazed
These are glorious days
Even though often lost
In some horrible haze
Endless maze
So many pathways
Does it pay?

There's no use being timid
Lost innocence needs tending
Our ways are bending
Unwise spending
Think twice, look nice
Consider heaven
You'll suffice

                    Spinning dice
                    My favorite vice
                    Has me crawling
                    Like wounded mice

Are you hearing my song or prayer?
Can you feel beyond a stare?
Do you care
        What's said of you?
Do you cry
        Because we're through?
What to do—
What to do –
Wipe the slate, begin anew?
Our words are few
Still wet with dew

Please frolic sunshine, tamper best
With hearts still locked
        In treasure chests
I'm a minor full of hope
        I'm an outcast trying to cope
Can it be? Can you see?
        What's the secret of the sea?
Drinking taverns filled with glee
Stinging crowds like buzzing bees
Am I quite the same as these?

A million stories to be told
A life that has yet to unfold
On must be bold
In a world still hunted by terrors of old
On new quests for gold
And rainbows
That can't be bought or sold

First I thought they were everything
Then I thought they were nothing
Now I'm not so sure

Every good poem must start a new page
The rest are passé so go forth
They all say
And carry on from day to day
Just like a play? I'm not so sure
What takes place between acts isn't proper to say
Success isn't fertile
True love isn't free
Push onward lost angel
I hope someday you'll find me.

My Boots

I just a flute
A muted flute
A fluke
A fruited fluke
A duke
A daring duke
Of muted flutes
And fruited flukes
And brutes
Brawling brutes
Brainless brawling brutes
That bruise
Flutes and flukes
And daring dukes
And other brawling brutes
That's what's in
My boots.

The Schoolyard

In the sunlight after school
Is where all the rules were broken
Is where chance was given token
Poking fun at those who took to heart
Lessons learned on classroom charts
Out here where lessons aren't as clear
Out here the lessons forever held dear

Snowballs, serenades
Baseball mitts and loud parades
The schoolyard, the schoolyard
Where friends became and parted
Where the fights and romances started
Where rivalry is championed, flowered
Dirty talk is worshipped, followed
Where through the grass there lies a path
That outgrows all the schoolhouse wrath
Out here where the whistle seldom guided
All the secret lessons confided

All is fun? Breath unscarred
Imagination, revelations
Animation, friendship fin
Swine is outcast ugly blind
Swine is spit on, kicked and tied
The schoolyard, the schoolyard
Only where the strong survive
Where weak seek to hide and die
While ghouls reap their prize of pie
The goody-two-shoes make

Nothing's shallow, nothing's deep
Nothing but the day will keep
Keep the treasures from the king
If strong he will come back again

Whether to be good or bad
Join the fad or climb a ladder
That is all that really matters
That is what the loud mouth tattles
Love is not so dirty, flirting
Innocent with something new
Good gum to chew and tell about
Hoorah! Hooray! A crown today!
Tomorrow's dungeon a day away
All together, forever change
A life has never more so starred
Than in the unbarred schoolyard.

Pops

Pops the dance floor's moving
With the music I am grooving
You scold me with your upper hand
But tell me can you see?   Have you
Had more fun than me?

Being young is so much fun
A non-stop game that's always won
I'm just a squire to the arts
Unruly playing life's game of darts
But I like the music playing
And live to dance when hips are swaying
Music's loud and I'm so proud
To be moving with this crazy crowd
And there's this girl in tight pink pants
She's the girl I want like mad
Dancing so crazy next to her I feel lazy
Me! Who's always on the run
She! Has my head spun
Back and forth her hips roll
Here and there her legs go
Her head just bobs in just delight
To my wild eyes she's such a sight
We'll get together later on
And found out what we're each made of
And Pops, Old Man, you're telling me
To grow up?
Just thought
Of being old
Makes me wanna
Throw up!

Pops I'm on fire
I wanna dance, not retire
Pops, the music's got me
Pops, you ever been so free?
Pops, I'm wiggling, my hearts pounding
All around my muscles bobbing
Throbbing, what a beat
This ain't no night of awkward heat
Colored lights are flashing on
The room is spinning and I'm on top
And Pops, Old Man, you're telling me
To settle down?

        It's the thought
        Of someday being slow
        Makes me never
        Wanna stop!

Gee Old Man
I'm sure you understand
I'm primed, I don't care
If you call me boy or man
I wanna dance while the music's hot
I don't wanna grow up and rot
Become an old fart fogie
Living a life that's full of
Hokey lines, living out
Exasperated lives pretending I
Am something that I'm not

Pops I wanna be loud
Dance hard enough to
Inspire this crowd
This woman's got me capsized
Won't dance with no one else right now
With any luck she'll take me to
The highest place I ever been'
Come tomorrow she'll be gone but Pops
(.....Phew!)
There's so many many more

I'm young Old Man
I'll do all while I can
You think too old
I'm tired of being told
Being called a young punk fool
Pops, live as I do then you'll see
Something besides
Your Golden rule.

For Leslie

The final platoon
Hummed a dark tune
It was a June noon
The marooned raccoon zoomed
Around the edge of the lagoon
Searching for mushrooms
Among the ruins of doom
Where a single prune
Covered the tomb
Of the groom
But whom was the loon
Harking for room
While a dumb bum
Drank rum
And strummed
For a stark lark
Leaving her mark
On the bark
In the park
After dark

      What does it mean?
      Ask the dead
      What he did with the lean teen
      Behind the screen
      He was a mean old bean

Hence
Even those
Who live in rented tents
Realize the wisest of men
Treasures nonsense.

Himexapigatroo

Himexapigatroo
    Belly umph!
Hanna rexxerana bwana
    Pop doogly shid
Hid cooble doobleda
    Tush scruffagus
Hippleflush
    Tump squnch
Hilshimery fun fung
    Ung inglemoo
Munst scrumkful bungaboo
    Tungle strundle-ungle-coodle
Bop pob mycliggelty stew
    Cung bellyscooter moddle wow
Hig pilly cow cow
    Sownburger stinglfirklefires
Dlinkenlcoker Coocrick
    Sew-eneye'll do
Goosecuddle hoggle woo
    Gobble goo
Finger funkin' out
    Pouty poonkleberry duffenhuse
Cruisin' Perry pomy stonks
    Himexapigatroo.

All Life's Lovelorn Days

I remember being young
      Running weightless in the summer sun
      Days were long and dreams were fun
      Until I beat the big bass drum

I remember roots and thorns
      Upcoming horns that stabbed the heart
      Left me bleeding on the floor
      Until new doors were opened
      When the child in me did rot
      Yes the summer sun was hot
      In cool Minnesota
      Where Pines as fine as apricots
      Didn't blemish reckless afterthoughts
      Until the drought steamed not serene
      Me not subtle but relieved
      In wake of well toned faded
      Glorious hymns of youth
      The tales were the greatest task
      Once the mask was shed

I now embrace the Frisco fog
      Red eyed like a deadbeat dog
      In gray and gloomy morning light
      I bite a piece of worldly pie
      And try
      To chew it without stinking
      Or blinking abstract arrogance
      Creating stares
      Like flashing neon underwear
      Unlike a lonely lumberjack
      Who has neither tact nor self-respect
      For proper principles of order

Louder
Whispering to the vacant walls
       Of decency cannot relieve
       The sympathy now shared
       For mystery inside the minds
       Of long dead literary men

I now do fear the racing clock
       The waves thrash at my aging
       Floating summer dock
       Mocked purposes galore
       I fear
       When one night interactions
       Do not sweep me off my feet no more
       Old age seems like such a bore
       Laced with weariness and worry
       I'm now in such an awful hurry
       To pick myself up off the floor
       Chase you round the apple tree
       And roll you in the grass once more.

Ode to An Ocean

Can you hear me
Lady of the Sea?
Can you feel me
I only want to be
Bright eyed
So I can see the world
As your slow tide
Takes me for a whirl

Treacherous waves
Take my boat to a shore
Far from this pier
I leave in uproar
Take me to castles
And unchartered isles
Show me true villains
Heroines and tyrants
Answer with robust
My adventuresome prayer
Take me to places
Most wouldn't dare
Build in me strength
The will of a hero
Breathe me free spirit
Unlike the sterile
Society's finest
Who shrink beneath peril

Hiss my sweet ocean
Crash loud your waves
I hear your calling
Your tide all obeys

Blow clear your fresh air
Calm cool my heat
Whisper sweet poems aloud
Wash clean my feet

Your power promising
To never end
Your rhythm draws me
Out to tend
To all the toils
I cannot mend

I'll never be
An ocean
Full of beauty,
Respect and dread
Powerful, but like a poem
You never end
Just lead way
To the horizon

Sailing further
Still you're out these
Where but the strong and lost
Are by the sea

In the wind.

Twinkle Toes

Twinkle Toes
Twinkle Toes
Laugh we all
At Twinkle Toes
But who knows
What makes her glow
And who puts on
A better show?

Twinkle Toes
No one knows
She don't show
What gets her down
Wearing a frown
She'll run and hide
Behind the bush
She cries inside,

Then Twinkle Toes
Comes out and glows
She puts on the best show,
And laugh we all
With Twinkle Toes
Who's act makes us
Forget our woes.

The Ballad of Timid Learned Fred

Timid Learned Fred
Never went to bed
Thought he'd grow his head
So all he did was read

Well, his wife Florace Blue
Didn't care what he knew
She loved him as he flew
But wished that he was through

His son Wild Will
Sadly mourned until
His Dad he'd like to kill
For the space he didn't fill

Timid Learned Fred
One day woke up instead
To find his son and wife had fled
He now sobs lonely in his bed.

Words, Days and Dreams

Words
Are only words
Wordy wordsmiths
Work your words around
The wisdom of the wind

Days
Are only days
Diehards living
Every day to be your last
Cannot prepare you for
Tomorrow
When you constantly accomplish
Nothing

Dreams
Are only dreams
Dreary dreamer
Dig your dreams into the ground
To seed.

If I had a dime
For all the endless time
I've spent just thinking
Sitting all alone
While hours roll
Astray,
Then I'd buy a day
When all of us could say
That we were all so happy
In every way,
But until that time
I'll just sit
and think some more.

Golden Goddess

Resting by a sacred pond
Beneath a patch of ivory blue
A girl whose hair was purely golden
Was leaving a trail for the curious few

"Follow me" she winked with her whispering eye
Disappearing so quickly I thought I might die
Her golden hair flowing on air to the woods
Gone behind trees from not far where I stood

Her moves so alluring, her shape so perfect
Her eyes so inviting me like fish to a net
I followed her into her magical maze
Searched every night for a great many days
Then I sat down to rest on a hard granite rock
And there for a clue was her golden lock

I felt rather silly, she made me a fool
Yet without her I knew that my soul would grow cruel
The sky cracked, a storm raged
Hard rain the sky drooled
I soaking wet, my ambition thus grew
Til' my temper raged like the violent thunder
My pace grew more hasteful over tree stumps I tumbled
I fought and I cursed and I searched til' I tired
Dropping near dead by the pond I'd admired

It was there then that the storm subsided
As trees lie fallen from stricken lightening misguided
That when I looked up a rainbow I saw
Beside which was that beauty with her long hair of gold

Too weakened to fight, to seize or to scold
I reached out my hand feeling old but still bold
She held it and whispered with her eyes glowing warm
"You've exhausted your youth but survived quite a storm."

As she lifted me up my weary bones grew back strong
Together we filled many nights up with song
We didn't cross the rainbow 'cause the colors were all wrong
Thunder growled in the distance
As we played for a long time by the pond.

The Quagmire

Anyways
Wonderful days
Multiply into a haze
Count the clouds or midnight stars
Or race the highways in fast cars
It don't really matter when
You're sinking in a quagmire

Hiccup psychedelia
Tantalizing barbecue
Changing anatomy in the attic
How frantic panic
Penguins painted inside
Stoned bones growing slow
Snorting snow
Springtime severs
Overdose
Drug bug narcosis
Squeezing, teasing, sleazing backwards
River serpents in the city
Trouble lit the candles
Blown out, away
One vast ashtray
Hot non-angelic nonsense
Under the hen a cracked egg lies
Talking egghead fearless
Meat cleaver coming down

On lovers under covers
Plugs, hugs
Forgetting the bedbugs
The rugs on the floor
Locked tight is the door
Envisioning more
        more
Enticing the horror
        Horror

Appetizing
The aftermath
A coldwater bath
Cooling the steam
Lost soul redeems
The sinking
Of dangerous thinking.

Two Old Aunts

Tiny secret
Weakened clock
Hidden locket
Weathered rock
Timid smile
Faded hoopla
Borrowed mime
Poor Aunt Julia

      Hallowed heart
      Horrid nightmare
      Helpless age
      Hopeful heaven
      Hindered speech
      Relieved duty
      Spoiled peach
      Poor Aunt Julie.

The Funnel

Principally platonic tonic
Never could remove the stains
Sounded out in stereophonic
Oh how sad those growing pains

Pounding out the principles
Grounded in the skull
Sharpening that new swift knife
Throwing out the dusty dull

Sinking solitude in songs
Of satisfying sight
Saddling up for flight
Into darkest night

Casting off the weight of wisdom
For the journey light
Hobbling in the shadows to
Escape the fire's fight

Journeying out to join the joys
Of outbound thrills and glories
Gory hangers on are trolling
Polling for some promised prize

Perhaps the best has yet to test
The race in space which all must face
A place to park proud in the dark
A lark to serenade each hark

Perhaps the master can't be cursed
With verses of such shallow vows
Ringing round the ruins of regret
For needless fights of fancy fret

A lark to serenade each hark
A place to park proud in the dark
The race in space which all must face
Perhaps the best has yet to test.

A Himalayan Albatross

A
Himalayan
Albatross
Hoppled to
The ragged cross
There he lost
His cherry pie
Where he found
A whole new eye
Now he hopples
All the time
Now he eats
All kinds of pie
And his eye's become
The boss
Of the ragged cross.

History
Repeats itself
And sits amidst the dust of
Forgetfulness

The Surreal Light Before Dawn

I awoke in the surreal light before dawn
To reassess my happiness
To contemplate the sorry woes of idleness
The fallen dreams of drunkenness
In the surreal light before dawn

The outside streets smothered dark in fog
I yawn inside
My castle, dungeon – Lonely luncheon
Watching past the others
Faded follies of fumbled foes
(*Oh, the woes!*)
And somewhere my toes found the power to drag
My untoned body out
Of the sloppy bed I slept in
After days of combed ambition
Seeking my addition into heaven while
The boys of hell were chasing women
Who laughed and ran with LA tans
And disappeared with rock'n roll fans
In customized vans and limousines and sportscars racing at
The fearless speed of night
While this I contemplated in the surreal light
Before another yawn
Wore the new day down

There was a clown, but not in this city
Such a pity, no wit and I'm shitty
While the mines of moronic minds
Twinkled at the drunkenness of pointless lunacy
I so blind I couldn't see
If the dreams had rose between
My hair-hid, half deaf ears
I hadn't caught the scent of such

The radio will play forever
If kept safe from foul weather
Whether my own bones can take such care
Or whither in the walnut walls of weariness
Or prosper in the palms of promised foolishness
Or crack in rebellion to blasphemous saintliness
I alone knew no such nurse for night

Fright then grabbed at my aching ankles
My bed led to sore of restless remorse
Upon the mantle was nothing but dust
Upon my brain was nothing but rust
Inside my hallowed heart lurked only lonely lust
Food was a must but I hadn't a dime
Nothing but time, free
To flourish my prime
The morning now lime, I
Shuffled my blistered feet to my desk
Where I sit in the surreal light
Before dawn's prelude to dusk

Can you see it for yourself –
The surreal light before dawn?
Or are you sleeping soundly until
The morning rays ripen
Alarm clocks have stricken the routine to rise
Open your eyes and where do you go?
Off to the hallways of one in a million?
Putting in time for humanity's halo
Or philosophy maybe has tightened your hold
And friends are merely obstacled foes
Who seek like you their own precious truths
You've got a polished tooth

I'm a convict in a noose
Running loose with crazed surprises
Mine eyes have seen no compromises
My ears have heard no lullabies since
I was merely a wishful child
Mild in all my merry ways
Until this haze filled my days

Locked me in this maze of mind and memory
Outside which I cannot
See
I drink warm
Tea
I fell the gains
Eternity
I close my eyes
Calamity
I breathe the air of
Inability to
Break this mold of
Destiny to
Find my own
Conformity, I
Blink and cry in
Agony, I
Stop and collect
History to
Quench my thirst for
Mystery to
Answer riddles of
Philosophy to
Find the self I
Want to be, I
Drink the vials of endless trials
And gaze at often-lively smiles
And crave to travel infinite miles
I laugh
Plot a path and
Crash into the day so dark
To stamp with brass my own true mark
To coin my sorrowed tenderloin
And join
The aftertaste
Of fast paced
Haste.

Paste me to the wall of choice
In hopes that I may have a voice
To shine alive with in dim hours
Communicate these riddles powers
And climb the everlasting towers
Unlike the waves of endless yawn
Thinks me
In the surreal light before dawn.

from day to day
skies turn gray
a few oases along the way
but mostly desert sands

The Little Black Spot

Sarah needed solitude
Sometimes more than others
Whenever things got hot she would
Retreat to her little black spot

Her friends began to wonder
When Sarah wandered more
Soon she vanished entirely
Gone through her little black door

Inside it was comfortable
Never would she want to leave
Then when she did she couldn't open the door
Now no one sees Sarah any more.

The Wasted One

Deep in the sun
The wasted one
Fried his eyes
Like a hot crossed bun
It was lots of fun
Those things we done
We always won
We drank a ton
But now there are none
In the sun
But the wasted one
And he no longer
Has any fun
Those days
Are done.

Laughing Juanita

Juanita hold
      Your ho-ho-ho's
For a whimsier time
      Not filled with woes
It's best to laugh
      Most full and true
But not at hearts
      All out of tune

I'll take you out
      To that ramshackle shack
Where we can giggle
      And scream without tact

But here the frost of death
      Has kissed limb
And laughter in its wake
      Cannot relieve the grim
Sorrow which abounds

So sip the scene
      And drink it down
Your laughter will
      Sound ever best
If you can add feeling
      To life's tragic quest

Then we'll go far
      Passed that ramshackle shack
Out where our smiles
      Will echo for miles
As our tactless laughs
      Triumphantly blast.

Outside of a Cookie Jar

It's early but I'm so tired
The weekend's through and I'm inspired
So many thoughts, so many dreams
Sometimes we want the world it seems
Yet we're so far away
From what we really need
To cherish what we give
The reason that we live
However far we travel
We cannot escape
The feeling we were born to
Inspire, gather round
Sometimes we have to lift, it seems
Our feet up off the ground
To blow away
Events that surround us everyday
To give our lives a break
Forget what's all at stake
And make love.

Monique E.

Kon-Tiki Monique E.
Hold back your cries
The world is on fire
So please dry your eyes
Your cries are so gentle
Your face sweet as gold
I'd just like to hold you
While we both grow up old
But there's fire in the homeland
Its' heat burns at my heels
Please Kon-Tiki Monique
Understand my ideals
I am but a poet
You are but my poem
Together we're a verse of beauty
Beside us there's no throne
A jungle's worth of dangers
A world filled with lies
That's what awaits me
Beyond your loving eyes
There are beasts to slay
More fired to tend
I as a seeker
My ways I must mend
I've not yet grown sober
True pride I can't send

Please Kon-Tiki Monique E.
Forgive all my sins
I try but I don't
Always let you come in
What are your pleasures?
Please tell my your fears
This time I'll listen
While holding you near

Kon-Tiki Monique E.
Hold back your cries
All of my words
Seem to sound much like lies
But feel past my words
Please search in my eyes
I am just a poet
Trying to reach for the skies
Inside me I'm human
Inside me I'm shy
Please Kon-Tiki Monique E.
Hold me tonight.

One from the Heart

It's hard to speak words
    When your eyes say it all
When your dreams become distant
    And your life becomes full
When you don't feel whole
    While part of you is gone
And your mind's not real clear
    But your thoughts make you smile

Like a dream
    Hours float astray
Whistles blowing softly
    From a hillside far away
Sunshine filling up the sky
    The earth bloomed bright in color
You wish you had a picture to
    Indulge your eyes while thoughts roll by

Lighter sing
    The sounds of crowds
Pleasant seems
    The world around
Warm and glowing
    Rich, enchanting...

Words aren't enough
There are none to be said
When the feeling is stronger.

Wind song

Breath drawn
Day will break
But for how long?

Windstorm
Mind torn
Who won't find
Their own true throne?

Wind blown
Heart thrown
In it's wake
Who will mourn?

The Wine Parade

On a raining
Summer morning
Here I'm writing
Drinking wine
On a grassy bank
Beside
A lonely pond haunted
By floating ghosts of fog
Frightening the quacking
Flapping ducks

Sing sweet pride
Soul not stride
Do not hide
Burning insides
Beside the light
There is no
Greater might

Out of the
Misty waters
marches a
Parade of
Startling
Sober thoughts
While wine
Loosens my
Cynical line
On time

Uptight
Bad moon
Rising in those
Steamy eyes
Skies are striking
Down the utmost
Penalty of nature

Hooligans
Sweet charades
Will savor from
This gloomy cage
Beside the stage
An audience applauds
Only the finest scenes
And act

Hipsters
Pranksters
Merry merry gangsters
Shoot 'em up
Knock 'em down
Bang bang
Ouch ouch
Let's get hip
Start the trip
Upon this glory
Expedition
Through the caverns
Mountaintops of
Life as it
Exists itself

Don't you come forth
Traveling, seeking truths
Without consulting
Older firms who
Drew more breaths, who
Conquered several jungles
That have since been
Turned to condos

Falling subtle
Drops upon
My splendid
Rendered pale cheek
Cold and meek
I like its touch

Hello hello
My generation
Seems we've slept through
Restless rerun afternoon
In front of the T.V.
Smoking merrily the demon weed
Seems tome its time that we
Stop lazing comfortably
And start to be

Apparitions
Need provisions
f the mind

Eventually I'll sail the sea
No minor misdemeanor
I'll now make
That epic fantasy
Unfold to really be
The truth of me

The midnight bog
Laced with fog
Home sweet home
To belching frogs
Who love their
Luxury: The swamp
In which we
Take our pee

This gloomy day
Would have no meaning
If I didn't
Give it one
I let the sun
Shine through my eyes
And burned some sleepy
Heads preferring shade
Instead

How far can we take it?
How long can we make it?
Is it good to fake it
If we cannot last
The marathon?

Crutches
Crutches
Always
Crutches

I'm alone and naked
Beside you I feel sacred
There will live beyond u
Mist creeps   Something of ourselves
Rain falls   Divine

Awaken!
Hear
The call before
All cities
Fall.
What for
Pouring rain   The rhythm reigns
Splashing pain   Will we
Where is the   Live in remains?
Shelter? Rainbow?

I do not wish to die, I reap
The harvest money will not buy
And death will cool my fortunes
Of effervescent life

So tall am I
In the eyes
Of a fly
Yet to the sky
I'm only a
Fly

I can criticize
All other's lives
But only in the mirror
Can I cure the lies
To right the truth

Rise up friends
Of Earth's
Last breath
Soon the skies
May echo death
War for certain
Cannot last
Past one more
Atomic blast

The sky is gray
As it can be
And I must be
A fool for sitting out
Amidst the soggy rain
Of falling skies
To Earth

But I enjoy
This damp sensation
I prefer it to
Dry noisy stations
Where spinning dizzy
Crowds do get
me down

It's really soft
the rain
Quite serene
and Sweet

If only I could keep
My pen and paper dry
I'd sit for hours
Soggy while
The sky proceeds
To cry.

I wouldn't trade
This morning for
A pound of gold
When it I leave
This morning's sold

Doors and Mirrors

Blocking
Reflecting
Closing
Opening up
Doors obstruct
Mirrors construct
Doors can shut out
What mirrors let in
Doors will frustrate
Mirrors will confuse
To pass a door
    You must open it
To cross a mirror
    You must understand it

If the door slams too hard
The mirror cracks
Shatters
Never to be
Mended

The Hollow Nightmare

Words,

            words

   Touch,

       touch

So much,

              much

   I hear an echo,

                  Echo

I feel so cold,

       Cold

     I must be empty,

                    Empty

      growing old.

Night

Fright   cry   chill
  Pills   don't   snore
   Bore   can't   peace
  Sleep   street   light
Bright   cars   race
By   squeal   honk
Cats   howl   foul
Prowl   out   in
  Bushes   dark   taps
   Window   fright   cry
    Chill   alone   quiet
     Tick   clock   tocks
      House   creeks   wreaks
       Death   goose   bumps
      Chill   fright   cry
     Night.

Children of the Moon

Mr. Moon,
In the nighttime, starlight bright
Deliver us from haunting fright
Just trembling children in the night
Crawling babes to our delight
Echoing our songs of peace
To violent lords who hear us least
For in the night we're all so small
Our terrors, from ignorance, grow so tall
All so weak, too strong to fail
We, nature's brains to save it all

Strong standing Moon
        Gleaming light from above
Please deliver us from
        Our fears not resolved
Our brothers are murderers
        Our fathers a lie
There are monsters in the shadows
        Who will not die
We can't cry
        Because we're strong
If we fight back
        We're just as wrong
I can't even trust
        My own self Moon
So please let me trust you

Faith is a healer
    Evil a desire
All us naked children nestle
    Curiously by the fire
The Devil's friend
    A world's end
What Moon weapon
    Can we send?
Flowers wilt so easily
    Diamonds do not mend
What the good is luxury
    When life has reached its end?

    Moonbeams, starlight
    You've brightened up this cold dark night
    Now soothe our minds so we might sleep
    Water our tongues and bury us deep
    In dreams of well tomorrows
    Dry tears of yesterday's sorrows
    Whisper poems of promise
    Bright ballads of joy
    Us children need these little toys
    Or else we make such terrible noise

        Thank you Moon and bless you
        And shine you on when we're all through
        To lead new children through the night
        Mending their wounds of needless fright.

The All Night Cafe

Here at the all night café
On and on the soft jazz plays
Tomorrow it'll be day – let it pass
The sleepy night will last and last
Free of fast paced headaches
Let the evening bake and swirl
Simmering eerily, easily breathe
Drinking warm coffee, smoking cheap leaves
Even the smoke floats slow and subtle
Outside the streets fight no rebuttal
Magically endlessly frozen in time
The stage light now lime, the crowd long cleared
Disappeared into dreams, in their beds they lay
While the rest of us dine at the all night café

Us reading, us staring, us snoozing erect
Us plotting dreams that the day will respect
Us sipping slow, us whispering low
Solemn as the night floats too far
Far as the solemn night will stray
Away with clouds of weightless haze
Dining at the all night café

Tin ceiling speaker plays
Voices mumble toneless astray
Smoke stems a surreal artists play
Scratching our ears and brains
Twisting our hair and legs
We're all awake
Thoughtfully begging the night tide to stay
Here after hours
In the all night café.

Sunshine, My Tai
Whiskey and rye
One more round and
I think that I'll die

Farewell Cold Brew

Twas evening when I awoke sober
What a slice of life had passed
Ah the merry melodies of summer

City streets still bright at night
A guiding light for those without sight
Blinded temporarily
Among bouncing smoky nightclubs
Some in fantasy, some in excess
For both the summer wind blows

Girls let their hair down freely
Curiously circling the fire to burn them
Also the ties that'll bind them down
They frown
           And move on
And the streets are filled with song all along
So those that shouldn't be anywhere near
Can justify no wrong

Over the bay floats the fog
Not on the streets where men can be hogs
Eating hot dogs
Barking and snorting and mooing in jest
A night's temptations are limitless
"Come sit awhile" some'll say with a smile
Soon they'll be running the home stretch mile

Then deep in the night
When the lights flicker out
Those not so lucky strut with an apathetic pout
Maybe a cigarette dangling in mouth
Hands so cold saddened in empty pockets
Until every sound in the street echoes lonely
The fog interferes with the sky once bright
There'll be no more stars tonight

One last breath steams
While the world falls to sleep
Night's carnival shuts down
The make-up comes off the clown

Walking through these empty streets
Trying to find home
Can't remember where I've been
What I've done or who I've seen
Don't know where I'm going to
But I hope that soon I'll find
That place I left with a frame of mind
Wondering about tomorrow
While I drank to yesterday
Is how I lost my way
Now I'm stuck out on these streets, full of booze
I got the 3 AM blues

Cold cup of coffee, still can't sober up
Wandering through these empty streets
No place to fill my cup
Eyes will stare, laughs will roll
But now they're all in bed
Still I'm out in unkept streets
I just can't sleep
Would like to just break down and weep
Don't wanna hear no more bad news
I already got the 3 AM blues,

Hence in the morning
Unwanted cold gray light
Some heads will be throbbing
Not hearts from the night

We bums will at once
undertake our task
Stumbling through life clutching
booze like a mask
By noon our world is fuzzy
Before the sun we're in the dark

These are not scum
But the self I've made
Who runs then whines
Falls dead stoned blind
Another gear rusting
In a town square clock
The sum of its parts ticking on....
Striking out time
No messages sublime
The day unclear is thine,

Then back to the night -- A neon party
Where repeated adventure quickly gets trite
Amidst it all somehow
Dog-tired I feel the bite
Of a simple slice of light set right

I awake somewhat
Sober
Without fight.

In The Dark

*

*

*

Ethereal surreal

Again in hidden zeal

Again somehow a meal

Again I steal moments from
The core that my peers don't explore
A part of likeness gone to ashes
What inspires will transpire
What transpires will inspire
In the dark

*

*

So it don't make sense *(Blah!)*

So I climbed the wrong fence *(Ahh!)*
And hid behind its' hidden pillars
Only caught the night's cold chillers

Well never does the day quite end
Nor heaven lend a helping hand
Time to move on

Groove on

Prove on

Blow the lid
And leave deep caverns
Dark with gloomy enterprise
Possessed? A Guest?
Or just a squire?
In the flames of worldly fire
Drowning at the river's edge
Before unleashed out to the sea
Of endless glee, more room to swim
So wide and yet inside so grim

*

Only in time
Because of the grime
The rest grooved on regardless
I now know the darkness
Climb I to the other side
Steep the cliffs that line the mind
Yet all does come together
In time

*

*

*

Sherlock's Song

Programmed sentiments
Sentimental alibis
Adolescent enterprise
Alimony intertwines
    Eyes of blue
      Words aren't true
    Who then slew
    Fang Sun Fu?

        Masterpiece of false charades
        Ruthless artful renegade
        Spaded the wicked ticket man
        Boiled his heart in a frying pan
          Sipping stew
          Villains two
          Are who slew
          Fang Sun Fu.

In Praise of Morning

I couldn't miss the morning
Not even if it stormed
I couldn't hiss the passing night
Instead I filed its thorns
I couldn't resist the deep blue sea
Beneath the scorching sun
Beneath the scorching sun I rode
To catch a glimpse of morning tide
To be part of the morning's pride
To feel a stride that others curse
Calling early morning adverse
A treasure let it now be known
Who's thrown my thoughts for such a whirl
I'd pass a thousand midnights for
And trade my chest of faded pearls
To join the morning's glow galore.

July

Ah how sweet the summer
Lounging lazy in the grass
Ah the peace, serenity
So much ease, simplicity

I feel the texture of the grass
The summer's royal brass
For long which seemed to me a dream
Now I'm on its throne

Ah the grass – a luxury!
Tender as the morning dew
Rich as heaven's sky
Bright as sun before the noon
True as Sunday's sleepy moon

All's in tune for the summer zealots
All the fruit is ripe for picking
All the trees blow sweet forgiving
Skies flame hot and bright
Such afternoon delight
With no loud gains
Nor binding chains
I feel no stains
On my resting pillow
All day I sleep
Beneath
The shaded rooftop of
This ancient willow

When I sleep
           I see
    A dream
        Enchanting
    Glowing blue
                    Sky at twilight
Awful haunting
           For more I'm wanting
    Other worlds, other thrills
                    Other's joys and spills

I in the green grass near Shakespeare's stage
Trying to see new light in the play
While the players for now are taking their bow
The rest of the crowd applauds
So what?
There's cheers be heard before
I've stirred cheers and laughs galore
Then the outline vanished around the cartoon
All the comics turned into real people

    That's where all
           My trouble began
    Once just a show
           Now merely a man

    These grains of new seed
    Blowing me out of the sea
    Into the flaming sky, I try
    To reach out unto land but
    My hands are tied to treason
    Entertainment tempts me piously
    I sip the sky and try to fly
    But all I create is ashes and dust
                    Ashes and dust
                         ...

Must my eye be a witness to sorry lots?
To impossible odds of entity?
To the dark paths where most cannot see? Where
Everyday I try and I squirm and I squeeze
Swinging from trees like blind chimpanzees

     Calling, crawling
            From the depths
   First I drool
        Then I sweat
   Whispering, blistering
     Awful debts
    What I act
     I quick regret

   Drinking those vials
          Was thrilling but weak
    I alone stood
        My bare feet in the creek
    My wandering eyes
        Preparing for dark
   While the rest were playing
      Content in the park

Can't you see people of the everyday sun
I'm not living just to work and have fun
I'm a thorn and since I've been born
I think it best to tear the page
Of common rage
Put to test the world's best
Not succumb to common deeds
Cherish goals of rotten greed
Heed that I might wake to breathe
New sight that obsoletes my guarded sheath!

     Arrogance
     No romance
     All bravado
     Stiletto
     Tomato ripe
     Pumpkin

Oven special
Chilled white wine
Puzzles
And principles
And promises of plot
Oh what a pitiful
            Sorrowful lot
Oh when the night comes
            Again my soul rots
And when the light comes
            I embrace it in knots

Why must life's mystery
            Unfold so deep
Into the realm
            Of such battered meek sheep?
The realm of sudden sadness
            The ruins of fallen entity
A lonely submarine
            Sunk deep in the sea
I'm all locked up
            In rotted woes
I've lost them all
            Loves, friends and foes
Fun, what is fun?
            I think that I've lost it
How without warning?
            When I so used to lust it
Fade me not withered
            In my own paradise
Send me no lies
            Nor old lullabies
These I do fear
            Are my sad summer songs:

            Faded promise
            Tarnished mind
            Passing through
            So many moods
            To deliver only

Obsessed odes
To half wit toads
Belching
Hopping
In their
Swamp

A nightmare yes
    Shall I retire?
A wilting aged
    Tending fire
Realizing I'll die
    So why the life?

I feel the drumming
A gray day is coming
Sleep, shall I
    Avoid its' doom?
No I must shine
    Devour its gloom

Clouds rearranging
    My mind is blazing
It's not that loud
    Nor proud am I
To bear those burdens
    Of the sky
My fast fingers playing
    A melodic piano
While inside they're feasting
    On everyday ridicule
Hoisting the minutemen
    I'm blasting off again

Here we go
    Recklessly wandering the sky
We be
    The lucky fools
We see
    No binding rules
Bed bugs aren't biting
    We dig the lightning

Eerie
            Experiment mania
                                    Hey!

                    Resurrection
                    Infestation
                    Condemnation
                    Blasphemy
        Imagination is the key
            Unlocking doors to infinity
    The mild ones, they sleep beguiled
            While at night the untamed beat
                    Goes wild

    Lost amidst my writing
            I somehow found it frightening
                            Then I saw the
lightening
    Lost amidst my writing
                                    When I saw
the lightening
    I somehow found it frightening   Lost amidst my writing
            Lost amidst my writing
                    Lost amidst my writing
        Running bare through a snow filled forest of white
            Where is cupid?
                                    Where is cupid?
        Running filled through a bare snow forest of white
                Where will my heart go wandering?
        Please!
        What trophies have I won?
        Why am I scared to swallow?
        Will I rust on this dusty shelf
        Counting on corners that haven't been swept?

    My hazy look of life sublimed
    I hear the wolves carousing
    And I'm full of tears
    Am I okay or just
    Subtly revolving around

Doorways of enchanted times
A child's nursery rhymes
Out amidst the cries of beasts
The hearty soul of night
The lights! Fantastic apparitions
       Heavenly dog bites
       Sailing ships of sadness
       Madness
       Crazy as a flaming match
       Soaking
       Toking nature's tasty fruit
       My head's aloof

Walking in the rain
I do feel not the strain
Of sitting down, being bound
To expectations of the roles of life
I'd rather be a bum at times
I often close my eyes
Often break the ties
Now I'm dry ·
More wry won't quench
My thirst, am I the first
To promise miracles derived
From my outrageous abstract remedies
For painful indecisions
Calling us a herd, I wonder
Why are we still yawning when
The dawn has risen in our eyes?

       Life has got dimension
       I need not to questions
       All the riddles of philosophy
       The ones that made me incomplete
       Ha-ha, ho-ho, hee-hee huh-huh
       I'll sit drinking at the bar
       Drinking to the summer stars
       While marching bands strike up a tune
       The big bass beating, loud brass blasting
       Proud feet marching two by two and single file
       And I'll smile, Lazing near
       Laughing on the pier

Waking up from a sleep so long
Seeing life beyond a page
Ah how sweet the summer
Forever blow sweet breeze please last
Ah how clear the endless sky
I'm taken by the spell it casts

I live
      Not like a solid board
I change
      To rearrange my sword
Blow forever free breeze of summer!
One day perhaps I'll blow free with it all
Or stand firm as I chose
Reviving serene such radiant scenes
By any means
I'll reap the prize of peaceful mind
Tonight
The evening clear'll be fine

      Ah, the summer grass is fresh
      I color, touch and smell
      I can taste, but I cannot hear it
      For unlike me, it makes no sound
      Blowing in the wind.

On the road
The dust is raising
Gazing still
Upon the hill

Corridors

Corridors where life's a bore
Searching for the right door
Walking in and out of all
Some make one smile, others fall

Now it seems its autumn
And there are few doors left
Now it seems all rotten
That the first door I left

Is it true another corridor
Lies beyond the final door?
If it's so then I best
Get comfortable in corridors.

The Rain Maid

In the rain
Standing wet head to toe
Is where I caught
Not a cold but your woe

Your eyes absorbed my rain
Yet like the skies you cried the same
I limping lame
We both proved quite tame

Mornings of laughter
Your giggling girl grin
Left me in sunshine
For a change I did win

Together so sweet
Yet a terror on our own
Remember –
Nights together hardly known?
So tragic, its casual
Inside so deep
We've both got others now
Though with none can we sleep
Easily
Without a sorry soul
Heedingly
In our lives there's such a hole

Then I saw you hiding
Behind your own tablecloth
After I saw you bloom
To the twitch of my mouth

Now here am I
In the pouring rain
You keeping dry
Your eyes wet just the same

Together
Would we ever
Complain to be sane
Or would we
Like rainbows
Glow after
The pain?

Little Girl

Little girl come knocking
My door, its always open
Little girl come calling 'cause
The sky is always falling

Little girl I'm crazy and
I'll never quite be sane
Little girl I need you
No one else will dance in the rain

Little girl I've dreamed of you
Little girl I've wept
There's much that I've forgotten
Yet your memory I've kept

I've wept and wept
Til' dead some nights
I'm not afraid to say
I'd sell a thousand wild nights
If your love was here today

Little girl come talk to me
I'm sitting by the sea
I'm sitting singing songs aloud
But no one's here but me.

Naughty Billy's Last Stand

Hung Naughty Billy
By his dirty skimpy shoe-strings
His middle finger signaling
A swear word to his savior

A smile on his face of triumph
He broke all hope of an alliance
Called it his last act of defiance
All the blood rushing to his head
As he hung upside-down 'til dead.

Purpose

What is poetry?
What is life?
Sing the melody
Sound the fife
A trifle of nonsense
An ounce of despair
A verse of some beauty
With wisdom to
spare.

Life

Laugh

Breathe   Sleep

                            Breed
        Stand

    Bleed

                        Hail

Drink   Win

                    Think
        Sweat

    Sail   Fail

                    Cry

To My Friend Who plays the Mandolin

You play your mandolin
But never win a tearful eye
You play both out and in
But never have you tried
To play your music for the crowd
No just to please yourself
I beg of you my shy, smart friend
To play your songs aloud

You move me with your melodies
Both sour and sweet, so silly and deep
You astound me with your ability
Yet I can see you're incomplete

Go play out for the toneless crowd
They'd shriek to hear you on the street
I beg of you my shy smart friend
Your public you must greet

To remain inside yourself, oh no
That's such a shameful crime
For if you cannot share your art
Your life is but an empty part

You will go far my friend
Your honor I'll defend
Your wounds with pride I'll tend
Your wrath I'll try and mend

Be strong my friend, I know you're shy
It hurts to hear a mocking cry
Yet what you spread ought best
To outlive what you dread
To live your life asleep in bed
In dreams of where your music's led
Will keep you lonely 'til life's end
I beg of you my shy smart friend
To share your songs with all.

Memories
A tragic thing
Competing with each day,
If they would go away
More we'd see
More would be
Yet more would spin
Ignorantly

The Battle Cry of Henry Bly

Ah shit!
Am I withdrawn
And left lonely in the dark
Memories of the park at noon
Memories of days bloomed full
Memories – beasts that drool
Rabid insects on the loose
Me a faded dying caboose
Take me to the fountain
        Where the fall of life is resurrected
Take me to the hideaway
        Where saints and pirates store their treasure
Free me from phlegmatic
        Incoherent senseless conversation
Roll me back in a four-leaf clover
Back where life began

I should have been a dog
Born to fuck and lye in the sun
I should have grown some crops
But instead I had such fun
Instigating trouble again
The police came around to bend
My way of wild perception

The fire wasn't hot enough
So I stoked it up
The night just wasn't bright enough
So I sang aloud
On the street curb on tiptoes
They called me drunk and locked me up
Again I'm in the dumps.

So the moon now wails low
And clouds intrude its gorgeous view
Of us here down on Earth

And then I met my friend
Who was saddened by each sight of day
He had so many tears and fears
It seemed they'd never go away
So I took offense
        Climbed up on the park bench and yelled –

            Scuttlebutt you hobo!
            Huddling helpless in the homeland
            Use the bones you've left and make a stand
            Infancy behind us now
            We can run the ragged route
            Or scheme on average dreams
            Or fuck off as we please
            Or strut the ponies to a small corral
            And ride the colts of high moral
            Another crazy realization
            Sound delicious? Sound divine?
            Again this nifty song of life

Life is such a treasure
Pleasure words cannot express
All that I have known
And felt
All the sights
And nights

Overhead the birds are swirling
Twirling free and easy mind you

Some days lazing
Under a bushy tree
Peaceful as can be
I watch the world spin round me
And try to reckon what I see
I don't feel guilty, don't feel sad
About the tree I sit beneath
Though I have little to bequeath
To my fellow man, but do they
Who speed around in cars so quick
Spinning circles round my walking stick
As I lay back
They race the track
But who wins in the end?

Maybe I'm quite crazy but
I'll smoke a cigar to its butt
And thank the man who made it
Thank you mister *Sale El Cheap*
Thank you ladies for such a treat
I'd give pearls to the world
If I had a clue, how to get a few

I see, I see, I see see see
See all that's around me now
All the garbage, all the flowers
In the center of the city
Spinning round me sitting calm
Wondering where I'm going
Knowing only round and round.

She was mine once
She was my only life once
She was my afternoon, evenings and sun
She was my everything, I was her one

We both had games to play
We both had dreams
We both had happiness
We as a team
We, her and I, were the pride of the league
We danced on starts and slept in the sky
We never touched ground, nor ever did try
Didn't see the days clear but we loved the ride

She left for the snow
I for the sun
We crashed back to Earth
Once we was done
Where poor Mister Moneybuckets hasn't got a prize
He's got everything but what
Money cannot buy
It seems he's lost his life between
Big deals and business scripts
Now his lips are lonely for
Something besides a dollar more

Echoing far out mating calls
Writing them down in bathroom stalls
On the walls that do divide us
Heaven help those who remind us
That we're only breaking rules
Making fools of those who care
I too am one of those, so there!

Saturday nights are slow
Everyone's dressed and joining a show
I'm alone and feeling low
On the curbs disturbed
By bragging
Warriors of the weekend

So I retreat to a damp old alley
Home sweet home, my home sweet home
The garbage smells the same
So looks the stone
Of my home sweet home
Dark and damp and nice
Only the mice to talk with
This is lost
A feeling
Spinning numb
A bum
Rip me off and
I don't care
Tear me up
I'll just stare

Help me oh Scuttlebutt
I'm in a sticky rut
Someone in the dark is killing me

I hear voices but there's no one near
They're whispering, I'm listening
I'm hearing things I don't wanna hear
Hold me near oh Scuttlebutt
The darkness now begins to strut
Across my face and in my eyes
The whispering voices aren't telling lies
Oh Scuttlebutt they're haunting me
Tormenting me oh Scuttlebutt
Scuttlebutt who can they be?
I am a strong man but...
Strangers I can't see
I can't call to invite for tea
Are after me
They want to kill my soul
Put my carcass on a pedestal
Oh Scuttlebutt my only friend
I truly need you now

Home sweet home
My home sweet home
The garbage looks the same
So looks the stone
Of my home sweet home
I get reminiscent
The city so distant
But lo! There's a moon above
Above it sours my heart like a dove
I smile all the while, smiling
Of all these trials I have to smile
I sing aloud
On the streetcurb
On tiptoes

Hear me out
A shout! A cry!
Open your senses
Before you die!

There's not a thing I long to know
More than the name of her who's glowing
Sewing stares upon her breast
Bedding cares deep down to rest
Ah, the time I sense has come
To finish swigging rum and dance
I prance among the giggling queens
To bright for any light it seems
And then I seek the princess right
The one who blushes with delight
As foolish me bow down to tend
To all her cares and pretty qualms
To her I'll smile and sing a song
And see if her heart is as strong

Hear me out
A shout! A cry!
I am drunk with more sunshine
Fresh air is the greatest wine
(Enhanced a bit by the bottle)

Instigating trouble again
The police came around to bend
My way of wild perception
They call me drunk
And lock me up
And that's the way it goes

Behind the melody I'll try
To make some good of all of this
All this endless bliss is filling
Me so full I just may burst

Mister officer Sir might I borrow
A dollar and a get out of jail card
I can't be imprisoned when
This bright new day is beckoning
I beg of you kind officer please
Release me to the world!

Instant Metamorphosis

A seal called me out to play
From his island hideaway
 But my kind I can't betray
By leaving on this troubled day

 Responsibility is a grown-up's pride
Scorns the leader of the seal tribe
 If you were a child you'd take my bribe
And sail with the free wind's tide.

Suddenly I realized
        Damn, I'm not a child
Instantly my yesterdays
        All seemed far too mild
Ahead the sky and seas looked wild
 So on my winter clothes I put
  And went to work.

The Artist's Plea

Singing a verse
That I've rehearsed
It's been a curse
The worst is over
Now that I've mastered it
Hand me your purse

Effervescent Ecstasy

I.

Neat?
I hardly think so
I hardly believe that you
    Have come to know responsibility
    As far as endless nightmares are concerned

I didn't believe in reincarnation
But I now believe that life
    Can die a million times
    And shine again as bright as ever
    As often as one tries

Christ
The absurdity of the bold human race
    "Don't touch me now
    Because I've got
    A headache due to traffic
    Caused by weather
    On this cursed morning."
Shit.

    Giggling in bed late at night
        While not remembering the day's routine
    Stay with me feeling of admirable ease
        Don't tease me with questions or opposing teams
    Or worse yet some stale pointless routine
        Where I'll have only one song in my head
    And nothing much new comes to
        To sleep in my bed

Run along the waves
                    Of yesterdays and thought tomorrows
Hollow admiration
            Only gets me feeling grand and lonely
Sand dollars on the shore
            Looking out to sea I want much more
Touch me
        Feel me
Don't believe the fears you often
        Pee out in the yard
The neighbors take it oh so hard

        Humble hallways can't relieve
            The noisy stairs you run to receive
        After righteous rituals which
                You laughed at bowing on your knees

                Oh
                The reigns of winter
                Ah
                The pain of existence
                Eeh
                The horror of violence
                Ooh
                The sorrows of turmoil
Fools of sorrow
 Don't forsake
The early autumn crop
 For zany afternoons of feast or famine

            I drink up
            I fall down
        I feel so much like a clown
    I just wish that I could enjoy it more
            Like I used to

                    Falling in the stew of things
                    Often times my head stings
                    With the soul that I'm
                    Still searching for

In the cold of night
　My nightmares do I fight
Hell is where the damned get cured
　　Or die alive forever
I wash my stink in showers coming
　Clean before the judges

　　You decide old man
　Is a young lad's mind
　　Full of fancy dreams that soon
　　　　Turn into desperate schemes?

　　What is greatness but an admirable trait?
What is life but a train towards fate?
　　If I think of but myself
　　　　But myself will think of me

　Curl your toes
　　And fancy that
　Prance among the garbage
　　Like a dirty golden rat
　Asleep with grand delusions
　　OF the way life used to be
　Giggling grins on summer lawns

　　Daylight dawns
　The continuation of
　　What I prepared for yesterday
　If I died it'd end
　　If I'm going to live I'm not
　Gonna moan nor piss
　　In the neighbors yard
　I'll have to give to keep
　　Some smiles saving me
　In an attempt that we might be
　　In tune like fine toned harmony

　Effervescent Ecstasy!

II.

And when I stop from talk the birds all sing
The air around me brings a breath
And I can but be blessed

With bliss of breath, taste sight and sound
To feel the firmness of the ground
Behold the treasures all around
Before my voice again drags me down

    A butterfly is dancing
        On the purple violets wild
    The ocean waves are thrashing
        On a shore so loud and violent
    A seal's voice is moaning
        From an island out from shore
    A stinging bee lands on my pen
        A dragonfly scares it off when
    The wind blows them together
        Under the ravishing sun

    I'm thinking of the beauty
        And what duty lies beyond
    As I lye whistling idle
        Near the freshness of the pond

Ye old blue ball is spinning
It doesn't matter who is winning
As long as it's still spinning
Around in space as it belongs
As long as we don't pop the ball
We will be winners all

    A devil in my left eye
        An angel in my right
    Without two eyes I think that I
        Wouldn't see so clear a sight

Kiss me angel
On my cheek
So I don't feel foolish
Walking meek

When I sleep I hear the dragon weep
And I pray for his soul to keep
The dragon – villain; foul and fierce
Pierced by arrows of the crowd

The crowd so loud they drowned his cries
They close their eyes to win the fight
While the beast of darkest night
Provoked does burn their children
Kill their wives

Will the battle ever stop
Or for all will the curtain drop?

The army trucks are marching in
To fight the dragons fire again
While the mighty beast in error
Wakes to breath his fire of terror

When the ground has been blown open wide
And the tide has washed its blood ashore
Finally will the door be opened
Only when we conceive the end?

Kiss me angel
On my cheek
So I don't feel guilty
Walking meek
While
Riding high the highways
Of instant satisfaction
As the world
Whirls pearls
Out into the rainy street
Where sun brained people flock to meet

Forgetting soggy skies and tears
 Forgetting to mark down the years
Drinking cheer and dancing
 Forgetting fears, romancing
Such a simple symphony
 Effervescent ecstasy
It's just a piece of poetry
 Won't bring riches to spread a mile
At best only bring an inner smile
 One that might outweigh the fears
        Let the music feel your ears
        And a message touch your mind
        When some peace will fill your heart
        Then will beauty fill your eyes

Earth and air
Sky and sea
Effervescent Ecstasy
The wine I drink
The song I sing
 All that I can think to be
My backbone, it is everything
It makes me smile
It makes me sweat
It renders me weary
 Then eases my fret
It's what I love
 Both work and play
My life flows on
 From day to day
Spreading it around
 In the streets the clowns
And jugglers bring a laugh
Human happiness – Joyous art!
Celebration!
Partying hardy in the alleys
 Where decaying stones survive
The lives that scratch them with graffiti

Good graffiti

Bad graffiti

All us leave our mark

On the walls that stand behind us

Of those that stand behind us
Will they dance a dream as we
Or live so sad to only dream to dance?

Kiss me angel
On my cheek
I get so frustrated
Walking meek

III.

I ain't sorry for my sins Lord
Not all of them at least
I'll answer honestly right now
You best to terminate my lease
If you say that unto you
I must bow and denounce

For I've seen glory in the night
I've growled with the dogs that bite
Though all I do's not right, that's true
Faultless saints I know are few

No one is perfect, *no!*
I know that to be true
Those who carry hearts of gold
Guard them proudly too

No one is perfect, *no!*
I *know* that to be true
That's what makes us mortals
Such an interesting crew

Dumb and crazy aren't we?
-- Wilder than the wind
Spinning round on our big blue ball
Yet I can't spin with it all
For soon I fear our ball may fall

The army trucks are marching in
To fight the dragon's fire again
The dragon wakes with hate and burns
An army yearning to defeat
Leaving no army to retreat

IV.

Is there no recourse?
Is there no remorse?
Someday there'll be just ashes
As the only remnants
Of the old world, cherished pearls
All burnt
All dead
It'll be sad when spring is dead
It'll be sad no seeds will grow
No one to remove the stains
No one to revive remains
Spring is now a pretty time
Spring is now a scene so prime

A time for tender dreams
            And young romances
A time for flowers blooming
            In the most outrageous   Colors

                        color
All to ashes

Must we sail these foolish seas
 To relive us from man's great disease?

                                    V.

                        A tender thrill
                            Just sent a chill
                    Up the back of my neck

                        She came close
                            I took a dose
                    We rolled around forever
                            Rolled in gold
                    Champagne and satin
                            Rolled back home
                            And off to heaven

                        Once I was a wild ghoul
                            Now I'm a romantic fool
                    First I screamed out battle cries
                    Now I've sight through silly eyes

                    Rock'n roll your engines baby!
                    I'm in love and I don't mean maybe!
                        Strap me to the gates of heaven
                            I'll not love like this again!
                                Without love
                            Where shines the light?

Without love
What's left but fright?
Without love
Where comes the might
To survive the day
Despite
The army marching on again
More weapons at the helm again
Just let the cursed dragon be
So we can all live peacefully

Pops the dance floor's moving
With this music I am grooving
Pops a good life's got me
Pops you ever been this free?
Pops I'm sailing, my hearts soaring
All around I see but glory
Pops I can't return your calling
Because deep in love again I'm falling

"Here comes the prince of darkness"
They scream
And the drum beats loud and scared
"Who will stand up to this lord?
Who will slay him with their sword?
Before his evil hand no doubt
Will flatten all to conquer."

I told them not to fight the dragon
The beast will live and die
More men are killed in fighting it
Than would ever catch his eye

They're rioting his cavern now
With torches, guns and hate
With a single breath he slays them all
From their flags proud call young soldiers die

Kon-Tiki Monique E.
I'm yours tonight
In the uncut grass
Beneath the foreign moonlight
The world feels so fine
Lighter sing
The sounds of crowds
Pleasant seems
The world around

Warm and glowing
Rich, enchanting
Together
We're a verse of beauty
Together, not alone
We've the whole world as our home

Thank you moon and bless you
And shine you on when we're all through
To lead new lovers through the night
Guiding their fearless eyes so bright

The army's marching on again
To fight the dragon's fire again

The dragon yawns and burns the pawns
New armies march on in at dawn

Without love
The music rots
Without love
We're sorry lots
Without love
The storm will grow
Without love
The lid will blow

I told them not to fight the dragon
The beast cannot be killed
It takes a beast to slay another
A new one then is born

They're stocking up on missiles now
To blow his home to kingdom come
They may succeed this time, no doubt
Ye old blue ball will then be done

Oh dear angel
Are you able
To come down and talk
With me awhile,
You've a smile
I'm on trial
Can you help me
Walk this mile?

Kiss me
Kiss me
On my cheek
I feel so weary
Walking meek

The violent hand again has triumphed
The tide has washed its' blood ashore
Please excuse my trembling sorrow
I can't bear this world no more

Ocean blue
Is it again up to you
To flood our shore
To save our ball?
Us who rule
Are still just fools
I guess we're through
Ocean blue

It'll be said when spring is dead
It'll be sad no seeds will grow

Who will stand up to this lord?
Who will slay him with their sword?

Angel kiss me
On my cheek
I feel my hands tied
Walking meek

The army's marching once again
The army's marching on again

Angel dearest savior
Bring on a brighter vision
I need nobler sight right now
To light the night that's framed a fight
For now I'm mad, a feeling prone
I want to smash a head

He will stand up to this lord!
He will slay him with his sword!

The army's marching on again
Getting my blood flowing
Good
Pumping my face red again
Great!
Steaming hot my head
I'm blowing up, jump!
Get out of my way
Though a calm dove by right
I'm a monster today
Do I scare you?
I dare you to try and attack
I'll blow up your shack
Get revenge and I'll hack to death
The part of you that I don't like

Hooray! Ha-ha Hooray!

Damn you Devil!
Damn you now!
As I curse, you laugh
That's just what you want

Sorry Devil, I've sad news
I'll just put out your explosive fuse
Your blood flowed through me today
But suddenly I'm better
Feeling healing from your breath
I heal feeling!
I heal touch!
I make the pain bit!
And cure with a punch!

Don't you ever change old friend
If you grow soft I'll help you mend
Without you I'd have been a fool
Without you life would be a bore
Now I'm right where I belong
Somewhere between sin and song

Throw up your arms boy
And I'll surely stab you
I'm seeding through you
You're good I'll slew
I'll make you a murderer
A madman, a ghoul
You will be perfect
You'll be my prize tool
Your head seems a strong one
It won't easy drool
Just wait until you see my boy
What you are when you leave my school!

Send me to your school old friend
I think it'd be quite fun
I endear forbidden pleasures
And I'll leave when it's done

I'll never be a saint
But I'll never sell your darkness
Tempt me with your joys of wrong
Serenade me all night long
I'll always be a friend to you
But friend and nothing more

Don't you mock the weak Devil
Who blindly follow you?
Isn't that why you grind them up
And boil them in the stew?

The world needs you Devil
You're an important clue
Without you'd there'd be heaven
With a lot of greenhorn dudes

Cry Devil! Fly Devil!
I do not want to see you die
There is both room for you and I
I see it written in the sky
So strong are our lives
Soon the lies will be forgiven

Down the showers then will fall
Tossing tears to all
Tears of sorrow, tears of joy
Grand scale teardrops falling
Glorious tears to all
Putting out the fire

VI.

No one was ever closer to
 The sound of death dismayed
No light is ever bolder
 Than where the sun's last body lays
No flight was ever finer
 No dream kept more elite
No temptation ever grander
 No melody as sweet

Through all the paths we've crossed
  And cursed
All the plays performed
          Rehearsed
All the handshakes, fists and kisses
    All the winds, all the misses
All the regret, glory, pain
    All the intimate pleasure ordained
All the trees we've climbed in youth
    All the stars we've sang beneath
All the swords kept in our sheaths
    All the fears, all the tears
All our wondrous years
    All have kept me in content
All regrets have been redempt
    And led me to the sea

          Effervescent ecstasy
    Shining in an emerald cup
    All the songs of yesterday
    Have changed as I've grown up
    Songs of pleasure, purpose, sorrow
    Songs of triumph I have borrowed
    Songs of ease, songs have pleased
    Led me praying on my knees
    Praying to relive disease
    Praying to stampede, release
    All the mirthful moments measured
          Out and mastered in a verse
    All the master's madness marching
          On, I mourn for mankind's curse
    All the deeds' all the growls
          All emotions good and foul
    All the people share the hour

          All the old men
          And ladies of the street
          All those in rags
          And neat ones elite
          All once watched sunsets
          And wept to themselves

All once missed chances
And wilted in peril
All once had futures
And dreams they kept clean
All once had vices
And discrete quick reliefs
All laughed in earnest
And nodded at truth
All laughed in ecstasy
And giggled in tune
All laughed once cynically
And bred a new ruin

Centuries of mankind's
Evolution
All dropped in our hands
Bouncing, bursting, ticking bomb
Ye old blue ball rolls near its tomb
Its face is mating with its fate
Ye old blue ball can no more wait
Wreck! Wreck!
The waves thrash the deck!
Pests! Guests!
We must save what's left!
The ship was once mine
        But now it is ours
The night started fine
        These are now desperate hours
Gentlemen! Drunken men!
        All please be quick!
We must make a miracle
        Or our ship will sink!
Quick! Sailor! Tailor!
        Lawman! Groom! Cook!
        Crook! Rich lad! Painter!
        You reading the Good book!
This is no time for prayers
        Promise nor pride
This is our last chance
        To stay above the tide

Heaven sure could help us
        If we were all dead
But since we're still down here on Earth
        We'll have to help ourselves instead

The army trucks are marching in
To fight the dragon's fire again
When the ground again blows open wide

The tide will splash its blood ashore

On the walls
            That stand behind us
    So behind us
                What will stand?

        Good graffiti

            Bad graffiti

                All us leave our mark

                Leave a mark

                    Our mark

                        Hark!

Loving angel
Let me kiss
My devil lips
Upon your cheek
I feel such noble
Wisdom fill me
When I'm walking meek

Humble horses
Clap your hoofs
Basement dwellers
Climb to the roof
Today the sun is rising
Rising high
There will be hope for you and I
If we try
I see it written in the sky
So bright are your eyes
Forgiven are the lies
Now the light binds us tight
Forevermore or maybe longer
Never have we been this strong
I see it written in the sky
So glad a tear falls from your eye
Forgotten are the times mistrusted
Now the stains are readjusted
Wiped clean the slate and nothing more
Opened anew is the door
I see it written in your eyes
As we head off to the skies.

aloof inside the cockpit
searching for the promised land

and if by chance a tear

American city
At sundown smells
of steaks and burgers
And looks towards comfort
                              on a winter night
Popcorn and cider
By the tele-
vision heat on high
Cuddled
in blankets and loved ones until
The tele-
phone intrusion   and out
                    into the wet crisp night to brave
     the unrewarding carnival, the street
                              those
                                        without
                              home without heat
                    entering
                    welcomeless
                         white
                         brick
                         walls   - sanitized
                                   - sterilized
                    to grasp a hand who's touch is
          faint

and if by chance a tear
                    should freeze to your face
                         on the
                         long
                    walk   home
          remember Earth knows no richer throne
                    than the bread you were bred to spread on
          the bed you rise to wave your vengeance on._

Molly

Christmas parties
Crusty graveyard
Goodness gracious
Molly moved,
Where she went is
With a stranger
Known to give out
Tasty food

I hold my hand out
On the corner
Molly knows me
Molly mourns
Molly sat down
In a sportscar
Racing off
For the moon

Molly's married
Molly's changed
Molly's marbles
Rearranged

No more message
Much more madness
No messiah
Big machine
Partly sailor
Wishful savior
Color crayons
Paint the scene

Golly Molly
Galloped onward
Off into the
Movie screen
In the bargain
Matinee I
Ceased to hear her
Youthful dreams

Come back Molly
Small town tinsel
Serenades you
Something fierce
Sacred sorrys
Aren't in order
All we've done is
spend our years.

Pardon Me

Pardon me but
        I needed this cigar
                        don't you see
        The rest of the world is smoking
                                        why not I?
        Silly how the bar
                                        flies
                High over heavy reality
Economics!   Pollution!   general imperfection
I'd give you a call
        I could deal with some affection
                                , but
                        the telephone is so impersonaland
                I don't have a fortune in coins
                        for every measlythree minutes
        Nobody loves a bum who calls collect
So I spent thirty-five cents
                        on a cigar instead.

Ink runs dry but
I've faith in the "close enough you can owe me the dime" sort
who'll
finance you a stack of napkins
and a corner booth to scrape your soul
People aren't so bad but
there's the world news
VIOLENCE and **WAR**
Black soot of exhaust, beer cans afloat
I'm smoking a cigar
instead of dope
and clearly the city
Swallows me up and licks its teeth with the sweet remembrance
of
my flavor:
Sweet and sour
Undercooked yet overdone

The meat tastes cheap   Yet
my blood was boiling when I flew
Long before the residue
Comsee, comsah
Taken for food
The modern world can be
Such
a machine,

But
If I hadn't turned back
out on the road tonight perhaps
The mechanical world could tonight dissolve
amidst
the simultaneity of
our longing,

But what the hell, let's face it
Nothing's so special it can't be replaced
I see beauty, lots of beauty
in this cheap old ashtray

I'd rather the truth
        Than some bland mausoleum
            Irrelevant sitcom
                Idiotic news

You should see how the smoke dances when it's unharmed
        Hear the leaves burn
            bewildered in my head
        Nothing makes much practical sense

Shoulda seen me on my knees
                        head in the shitter
            Not so awful proud no more
        from repeated dreams of death confronted
I see humans as high tech mice
                            Seen a dead
man on the floor
                In the Oakland BART station the night
before
    On the way home from empty hours of pointless conversation

        Truly I'd call if I were drunker
Truly I'm not so burnt as I seem
        Seldom so sober actually
                I've pleasant dreams
                    I've thoughts of you
        Your name, shape, frame of mind, unique delight

        I'm not unkind, I still fancy
            A picnic by the sea on Sunday yes!
                That would be fine
        Now-

        Onto the marble world
Polished
        vibrant
            vague, Full of
    Fantastic delusions Conformed to
by unoriginal creators of guilt.

Long Road Home

It's a long road home from Hollywood
There's a lot of make-up to remove
to leave the acting and the glitter
and bathe again in spring drawn water

There's a lot of lies to rectify
a lot to quick explain
There's a lot of care in apple pie
and a lot of tears in rain

It's a lonely road away from home
but it's grander filled with dreams
Each step back home is painful
returning to reality.

Beneath Bootstraps Discontent

Counting highway miles beneath bootstraps not content
evening nobody lies down watches news and sleeps
twang country negro blues ticking heartbeat precious
rural town small u.s. polka one night stand and off
the sound of tired children
                                          worn out with ordinary gains
raindrops strange
                              cleaning premonition
rushingspeedboat spit in ocean, tables vast and turning
fences erected, confounding bridges, burned
words words and yak yak yak who or why
where we came and doom explode spanish guitar
over backwards ever belly leaking flop aching brain
on and on again time running and love
whispers

again again and time again
                                          and clearly
the sewer lights the welcome sign
roots of prime time satisfaction
titillation trying
                                    diving beneath biscuit moons
jumpin' static out of lip sync
around the maybe world losin' risky formal nametags
poppin' worlds down loud   guitar proud twice and never
                      chicago deco
streetlamp sorrow
                                                nightlife sax
                    intellect beardless
                                          conservative sellout
back to where boys turn bald loadin' flour bailin' hay

enter town pump easy small talk
jumpin' out of toilet bowls to gargle projects precious few
aghast with pre-dawn sorrow

            alone at last

hard reasoning accepted telling shameful wonders
shimmer flash in darkness armless deceased race
                                 rise up again
no crash inferno evenings no
rock and roll salvation twist and bop out of mind
hurry relax pop lid get hip togetherness cha-cha
my masquerade my color
adding to the gray world beautiful
shakin' rockin' hollywoods scratched up imagination
take to the air city billy, take to the air
stop flashing art brilliance
changing changing love vacation
never promising future heavens
upgrading
pet parrots talking riches plain

Fog and Wind

Fog sneaks silent in
With Pacific wind
Away my love away
We shan't be shadowed by dismay
Our time, our touch is all
Beyond this magic hour we wake
Alas, I feel a shiver
As well do I feel birth

Away my love away
Try I will to catch you
Peculiar aren't the premises
Upon which our foundation rests
I ask you, What makes sense?
Passing among relative mysteries
As fog sneaks silent in
With Pacific wind

In a new moment of height, we rise
Expanding abstract vistas
Encircling beauty in all we see
We waste, we touch a melody
Away
My love away
To paint the faithless with such wisdom
Our time, our touch is all
Our coming sleep must hold no secrets.

Hissing of an Unsung Bum

There's someone sitting on the steps
Whom few will ever know
Old glory'll rise above him
But no harmonica accompany his melancholy woe

On urban sun drenched streets he sits in rags in shadows of hope
Dreaming of days when life was richer
In a big old house he lived in
In a far gone world with which he could cope

His eyes fade in far gone memory
Now the sun's a luxury
He's the end of the family tree
Claiming too proud for sympathy

Richer man walks by ignoring his smell
As others strut passed and spit on his well

He's a friend to all the insane
Deranged crazy madmen with bottles for brains
Old winos who've never known complete ends
Desperate losers who'd kiss the devil for gain

In a hazy late afternoon sweat
He gets up from the steps
To cruise forgotten alleyways
Scraping for bits of substance to
Sustain him through the cold soul of night
Until a new dawn shines it's light
For him to carry on
Gainlessly
In his estranged lot

There's little time to buy, says he
By fretting through the cold of night
Bargaining for petty thrills
There's not so many well-stacked tills

A hero needs no throne of gold
Wouldn't stand being showered with rewards
Until his limbs grow weak and old
He wouldn't stand under a saluted flag
Collecting praise like a bum collects trash
In a paper bag
Sitting idle hearing songs of his deeds
No instead he's in the shadows
Unknown and on the run

That's what says this man in rags
sitting
at the top of the stairs
In the sun

So bums we all
Do heroes rise and fall?
Struggling with pain while we point our thumbs in vain
Running to escape the rain we drool
Aimlessly floundering
Stumbling blindly through and passed
What we never saw or knew
Left insight alone for the few
We bowed to on our knees
And drank to their bold feats at our own ease
Before ever questioning our own disease

Our temptations divine
We wine and we dine
Our spirit doing little
But just marking time
We never fly
Never grow tall
Only criticize
Instead of knowing the depths of a fall

Who of the famed intellectual brigade
is taking a stand to start a parade?
The sharp ones earn paychecks
The rest read good books
Some survive on just their good looks

But who's really living
        and breathing the air?
Who's life means more
        Than their fancy hardware?
Luxurious elegant, high status junk
Lock it all up in a dusty old trunk
Then can you stand solo as a human who's higher
Than a starving trashed bum in streets filled with fire?
Are your ways worthy of another fast buck?
Or do you owe your whole life to one stroke of good luck?
Have you worked? Ever suffered?
Have you shared yourself with others?
Are you sorry? Are you sad?
Are there things that make you mad?
Is your life a changing fad?
Can you cope with other's hopes?
Or do you only climb your own high ropes?
Does depression get you down?
Been insulted by a clown?

Wear a frown or do you hide it?
Smile when happy or be frank despite it?
Can you give in to a melting warm grin?
Are you bold enough to withstand a punch in the chin?
Do you only want to win?

Then when one stumbles and falls
Removing his name from all hallowed halls
It's not the end but a miserable ride
A slide beneath the accepted stride

It's those who feel the darker days
Who learn their moon and how to glow
Who know that life's not just a show
Through pain one feels
A need to heal

Our brains made of richer bottles
Expensive dress and fancy junk
Our life is faster, our faces more sung
But how much nobler than an unsung bum?

The Rain

The rain falls pale
 from under my veil I watch
A storm creeps shallow
 from out of a deep sleep I move
Ink is running
 blurring the words abandoned
Noon is calling
 wondering what the delay is,

    Ruins of the party
     sicken the stale smell
    Blooms a new premise
     needed to widen the shore
    The moon leaps gallant
     and why do I wonder what for?
    So soon naps the sparrow
     shivering under the sun

        Forward into battle
        Jesters incorporate their wit
    unto a moldy arrow
         None but the hour will know
        But it will grow, Seascapes slide
        Dive the doves! Dive the hawks!
Fly the fair!   Fly the foul!

      i wipe the rain with a towel.

America

America, I fear you're settling
Into a comfortable oblivion that will not grow
You have to have your cars wet bars and tv sets
Recliners, slippers and dining room sets
Have to keep those cars waxed
Pay your insurance tabs
and keep the house locked all the time with the radio on to scare
      away the burglars with the AM news

     America, are you full of fear?
Is knowledge harmful? Do you trust your neighbor?

       What about eternity America?
          You've raped your mother dry in places
Hoarding the wealth while elsewhere the world goes without
food
     Closing your eyes with your arms on the world
               Your youth is faded
      Does that refurbished lady still hold hope?
    Is comfort worth more than truth and decency?
          Will that new toy enrich you so?
America
 are you just a dream
  that bounds together all the roadsigns?

Home of the dollar, Trains and Tv
    striding for glory
Thanks for the memories, sorry about the heartache
Racing proud the **FREE**way, trying to do it **MY** way
          while the immigrants keep stealing in
in search of the American self centered dream

Your kids go to school to get a degree
 They cheat and don't bother to learn anything
      Get off your blind righteous pride America!
      I think you pat yourself on the back too often
You let your minds grow awful numb
Watching the same rerun plots
Shifted in different time slots

Remember history America?
You hate the Russians but don't know why
Because the President tells you so?
What about the mush-heads who agree with anyone?
Or dogmatic righteous bores who have no ears to listen?

Do you know what your neighbor thinks?
Do you know your neighbor America?
Do you know who you are America?

I am America
I am the meat bones mind and fat
I am the hustler, I am the scholar
I dream and I work and I work and I dream
I sweep the streets and I litter them to
I'm progress, pollution and POWER
The flagwaver proud and dogmatic
Raising my fist claiming God's on my side
I was bred for consumption, profit and pride
I declare loving freedom, but define it not
I criticize what I do not know
I talk loud, I conquer, I own
Ignorant, wise, I seek truth and tell lies
I am the left and I am the right
The raped indian and the slave trader too
I've a voice to heckle authority
And a pocket of dirty money
I'm a transient in a seedy urban hotel
A millionaire lounging out back by my pool

the stage
is but a race
for **me!**
at the finish line is
luxury.

I struggle to get by
not prim and proper, I don't drive 55
I don't trust Russian politicians anymore than I trust
American politicians
I don't trust politicians.

I don't think we're God's only nation
I don't believe the President
I mistrust salesman and rhetoric
I like small towns and apple pie
I struggle to get by
With friends who snort cocaine
Who sleep with their bosses to get ahead
Who go to church who
cheat on their husbands and wives, who drink too much, who are
gay outcast hippie yuppie foreign alien derelict assholes and rich
bastards, poor suckers, fuckers, priests, musicians, democrats,
republican radicals, bartenders, hookers city slickers freaks and
hicks,
I don't agree with them all but I try and love them
Some more than others
Give me your hungry, your needy, your sick
Throw back your full of shit hypocrites!
We're none of us perfect, none completely correct
Too much flag waving not enough thinking
What about the rest of the world?
          Are we friend or invading foe?
Do we keep our doors locked in suspicion?

                    Do we know what's beyond our walls?
                                   Do we care?

          Look in your mirror and stop lying to yourself
Show a little humanity
Have empathy with your enemy
  Be skeptical America keep score
Sorry if I'm cynical I'm not blind
I'm not a muckraker, I want to be an artist
I wanna help design a world that will last
I'm tired of bullshit America
I care about a life that isn't fading
Into pudding pie so neat and unquestioned
I want to be the neighbor of an open mind
Ideology and economics are for discussion not death
I won't die for them
I won't burn the flag but I won't wave it stupidly
I'm most critical of myself not my enemy

I want to make good
Here at the genesis of fifty thousand generations beyond
So much waste with Earth getting scarcer
Quit putting yourself on a pedestal America
Wake up and discover what you are
Such big muscles in your arms
What about the space between your ears?
Your untapped resources? Your bulging bellies?

You live for one, you live for many
You live in search of plenty
You lie, you cheat, you smile, you whisper
Your heart and mind compete

Sometimes after lines are delivered
Do you wonder where their meaning was?
In keeping pace with mealtime
We all allow for that what feeds us

Faraway dates don't deliver
I've felt that pool of promise drain
Spotlight on your eyes that wander
Where do you wish to be found tonight?

Always do we ask for more
Off across the sea with smiles
Miles trampled
The whole world glows
Always complaining but seldom creating
Everyone cuts their own peace or they try
baking more pie for a slice in the world
or dying and not knowing why

And when all is said and done
So much is said and little done
Little wars are won
and bigger battles wait

Should the sun not rise who'll be at fault

Those who resigned, or those who put it out?

Seeking to rock the ship, to make it stronger
A hooligan rebel wants only to rock
While slipping on smooth through the trials of time
                    a cool cat escapes dimension

Bludgeoning on through the trenches of time
        There is no rhyme, Uneven heaven
                Pale reminders and mildewing bookbinders
Fastened down firm by the bootstraps in protest

                    Scholarly pilgrim lost in abstract worlds
            Adventurer knowing only where he stands
Warp the two together and the universe expands
            Decently, learnedly, apart from the masses

                        Civilization, so weighted and vast
        A field of ants in a backwards rural country
Bludgeoning on through the trenches of time
                    With no linear road, relative to no one.

Unaware

cloudless sky

underwent few changes

through the ages

passing

strides are lasting

song is

changing

unaware

I stare

at yesterday

tomorrow

off

to nowhere

baldy

Scare you baldy?
Asleep at the automat
I get vibrations off this lunch
Chummy mustard, wet baloney
It says here there's a tour
To the mountain where Moses received
The ten commandments

Graffiti in the Men's Room says:
Steer this battleship to that party heaven
Far beyond this Nuclear sundown

Have you seen the news?
There's a war going on somewhere near here
But don't fear
NYC is indestructible, just like
Captain America
And this chick in the centerfold

Baldy...can you spare a quarter
For a renewal of my spirits?
The fall fashions'll be in soon
If I can just look cool til then

I saw
A cigar smoking steer in a limousine today
And last night cold cats careened from the fence

I love this set
Let's make it a scene
Tie it into the plot and we'll have
us a blockbuster on the ballot

Baldy--
Did you hear what I said?
Or
Did you put all your membrane into the slot
and got no change back?

Now we know
    About siblings and currency
    Democracy and outer space

    At the beach
    Behind sunglasses are feasting eyes
    Cool, hidden
            A metaphor
                          for
                The chosen and their ilk

    Silk stockings, macho cologne
    Man,
    I don't wanna own you
    And I don't want you to own me

    The sea
    Fills our heads with the sea
    A shadow of the dinosaur on the sand.

and Cold at Night, Western Culture Dreamless

Bald balls
Clean dolls
The news says curse
Reach in your purse
Or you won't be either
Happy or hip
Well shit,
On such a hot summer day like today
I don't see why it'd be a sin
To walk down the street in my birthday suit
That I'm not ashamed of, and frankly
I can't figure out why society
Seems so damn shy of revealing itself
What are they hiding?
Are they afraid to discover something?

I really think it's warped
To keep children seeking nakedness in secret
   forbidden glossy magazines
Is there something repugnant about the human body
         undisguised?
Are we so ashamed we must keep ourselves covered up?

                    I, for one, am not ashamed

Educated? Liberated?
Seems we're going backwards towards
Stone age ignorance
ME vs you
Prejudice and patriotism
Greed and violent problem solving
Weird illogical ideologies
What happened to the revolutionary spirit?
                              Pioneers of the world!
Instead of turning the world on
We fuck it up
Worshipping art, neglecting truth
 dissecting myth and ignoring history's lessons

A tool for master con men
Freedom is a vulgarized word
A slogan for egos of ignorance
What does it mean?
A nation of spoiled, short sighted sheep

Does nobody dare to soil their hands
 by digging beneath the surface to see
that the alter of praise is built upon
the blood of our sisters and brothers and greed?

            and cold at night, Western culture dreamless
Ignores deeper visions
 Waking on a crowded city bus on a raining rush hour morn
 Gut aching from coffee
The day like a stale, invisible sandwich
 Which'll be eaten regardless
 and hardly tasted

Who knows freedom?
                    in faced paced routine, convention clean?
             thoughts passed on from mind to mind
                    Where do they all derive?
Bald balls
Clean dolls
The news says all is right
Sleep tight
Think not
Someone saintly's at the helm.

The Wake

Someone help those tears
Bleeding now for long lost years
The fear of death is stirred in all
Eyes closed I picture waterfalls

A smell of sickness fills the room
A winter cough, a child snickers
Verses of blessings read with hope
But afterwards, what's dead is dead.

Down By The Docks

Down by the docks where the timid don't go
big busted women
and Irish whiskey flows

Waitress sings a song, piano player knows them all
as the bar boss steals kisses, but the girls aren't out for practice

The place is rich, ceiling low
They call it sailor's row
The floor is slanted down but tonight is looking up
Lights are dim and walls are crusty
Sailors from the sea are lusty
Smoky small talk, accents vary
Toast we all to nights of fury

Any song you name that piano player knows
Any game you play you better know what goes
Blondie with her warm legs finds a starved man for a bill
Kind sailor's girl on purpose quits her birth control pills
Badass in an instant stands to challenge his crown
Balding sloppy loser stands to knock another down
Grinning, a young lad thrives on the thrills
To him the night's chills are really not there

Big bar boss shouts a curse
Badass gets offended
Black dad in his fur coat
Gathers up his girls and leaves
Grinning young man's eyes awake
In his hand performs a shining blade
As the balding man, martini in hand
Stands to sing religion
A gallant girl with gracious breasts
Caresses her arms around the young man's chest
All calm down and the show goes on
Bar boss serves another round
and the piano player plays on and on.

Children of Catastrophe

How can I sleep while the bomb ticks on?
What kind of fools are they or am I
To live with a bane that will end all our lives?
So inhumane it's completely insane
To let such madness reign what can we be
But children of catastrophe,

Did we make this? Our superior race
Each moment it waits to blow life into waste
How can I drink or dance
Or think of my own selfish path
When by the morn all may be gone
How do we sleep when the bomb ticks on?

Dawn may shine on none but ashes
Did we make this? Our superior race
Each morning I wake to our epic disgrace
I'll take a bath but not be clean
Still a child of catastrophe

A Lullaby

Sleep tight America, sweet dreams

there's no world on the news tonight

A cat in tree, two Local madmen

sport's scores and some weather

Hush hush sweet lullaby

Sleep, sleep until you wake

rested anew

we'll meet in someone

it matters not who

Love universal

interacting, feeding

Relieving the deep fatal wound

dream but do wake and see

no illusion.

The Modern Mountain

forward

You won't get away
  saving your pennies for someday

won't get a head
  counting on idle bedridden dreams

              or so they say
                with much dismay

I've seen
  and heard their vulgar justifications
    and pure, know

that once their poetry was heaven.

1.

The times are **MAD**[1] I read today
Grist to the mill, Anchors aweigh!

half the sockets missing bulbs
Pleasant dreams to your children.

It's not the heat of the night
nor the brightness of the sunshine,
Only the waking hour's ounce of mad thoughts
Rising up between your ears
Tell your peers that, play your fiddle swing your bat

I've hung loose on all edges
Smoked Benson and Hedges
Fought the dragons for the ladies
Then picked at the prize like an evil raven

So much liquor in my head
my head is dead

the look of love not glowing
I'm in transit

Dogs fighting dogs for food
Impartial to the news

Now sun creep up, I cannot hide
day is calling out again

---

[1] **Mutually assured destruction (M.A.D.)** is a doctrine of military strategy in which a full-scale use of nuclear weapons by two opposing sides would effectively result in the destruction of both the attacker and the defender.

Footsteps in the distance   Waves of an eternal sea
              Old movies on the television,
                      What else do you know?
          Those who cling to vines
No more than a grape will be
          the rest of us go beating our minds tiredly.

          One line may be beautiful but not worth a lifetime
What difference does it matter?
          Snowdrifts bury autumn beauty
                  Brilliant lines that never fit
Fade

  In the whirlpool there's no plan
      Only beauty in its science,   It's
                                        all the junk
                                    that we recite
                                that makes up most
                                  Our World

                            It's all the junk
                            that clutters the brain
                            that keeps us oft
                            from seeing

              It's all the junk
              that clutters the day
              that makes us incomplete

  If we wouldn't compete
   Use only pure devices
  Perhaps the sun and moon would
   be our favorite vices.

  Skipping back to simpler days
      When melodies were better than realities
     Then moonlight meant much more than money
       Cocktails were an adventure, not a curse

Now the noose slips on too easy
in that sleazy shack out back
Your dress
a little daring, yes
But what about the Earth?

Youthful smile in a timid manner
where went you Timmy Slater?
all the world was such a farce
Til slapped strait once too often
and found
The treasure buried in the ground
by pirates of time, wizards of knowledge
Who filled the garden up with lizards?
Snakes with fangs that hunted doves
While us flowers
fainted
Painted
Now the scene is not clear
dated
It's another year
Another round of bullshit
and more beer
Something wise must leak in the skull.

Hopeless clowns go frowning
through days grand illusions
Losing
whatever happens
Cruising
too fast to contemplate
Fate
while I
with both feet on the ground
was sailing on a sled down enchanted peaks of old
Stumbling towards the fencepost
another board to bang my head on
wondering
Why seas were swelling
wondering
seas are always Swelling

sun creeps up I cannot hide
Day is calling out again

Girls go riding bicycles on easy street
their happy figures waving
Sunshine breaks the clouds but promises to leave

THUNDERING
Will the thunder bring death?
Could this moment be our last breath?

All these fine sensations
over?
How can I sleep?

the glory of the moonlight
doesn't mean much anymore
Hungry
I don't know what for

Launching
another backdrop in the alley
trying to breathe another breath

of Reality.

2.

Were we ever there   or just ?
sailing in and out

Wondering about the high seas
while wading in a pond,

Oh yes quite on a voyage
off to places far from day
is why today raced by unnoticed
and why life seemed less than a play

I can drink myself to oblivion
just to bloom with life again
But that won't ease the thistles of the morn

Storming out of routine
tossed
among open air
Reaching high for hideous insight
mother father preacher
and the garbage man were teachers
a jester in the bleachers
Life was somewhat of a marvel
Love was laughter rolling on the lawn
believing life was but a song
drilling holes in roads for pleasure
Until the pleasure took its toll

Youth was glory
youth was fun
Does age bring meaning?
Purpose?   Love?
Or is that all
bullshit ?
What's beyond dreams that transpire?
Hard the rain that cools the fire
Who were we? Where did we go?
Once us buffoons were king!
We drank to anything
Our optimism blending with our frolic while we learned
of life in fast backseats
Our music blasting loud and   proud
While making fun of teachers scolding
We drove the cops all to their limit
Threw our fat food just for fun
Way up high on the roof of the world
Under the moonlight trading magic

Sleepless nights and days
        off the cliff of self control
Never thought much of the morn

Can you still hear
   that wild loud rock
      n'roll?   How it
                  shook our limbs, possessed our souls
            and though the show seems simple
   There were depths behind the curtain
Concealed from all the laughter and applause,

   Now the bird that's flown that nest
   Must've missed the final scene
   Suddenly, alone it seems
walking tall on sober morns to conquer yet the wind

         seems we've scattered, sprouted
   Standing   as the world spins round
      Home at last I hear the echo
         of the last O.D.

            After that the party kings looked foolish
         Some died staring into television screens
      Fell in pits of routine with business degrees
   Or screaming last defiance on a drunken highway cruise
         The playboys soon got married
   Misfits all found their place
            The Animal House is silent now
            shipwrecked on the shore decaying

               We can't set back the clock
            Can't recount the winning's lost,
            Once atop of carefree mountains
         Once the surfers of the tide
   We hit shore stoned running for but glory
   But there wasn't much in store

   In our hearts what is it we adore?
Has the ringing of the clock murdered our life-blessed souls?
   Our faces, still so young, now reek experience

and here it is another year
You're over there and I'm over here
No more tossing money to the air
Drinking dancing effervescently enhanced
Now reigns a loud silence
Between thoughts we won't expose
Now it's hard to touch because we
sleep with others who are not the loves we had when we
were young

Once we kissed and didn't question
Now we dine on wisdom's wine
Take time only to step high
Now our beds are dignified
but do we dress each morn with pride?

Yes'n how the fire flickers
When the wind comes creeping in
and do I hear my heart shiver
as each flame dies and begins?

It's been many moments now
Since we've killed the golden cow
Since that widowed sow hath wept
Since with nightmares have we slept

It's been many moments since
The piper played his finest tune
Now wind blows swift past Lancelot's tomb
In her womb grows Mary's child
She walks alone the forest wild

A political antagonist, bellringer of doom
Once I sat in the rain and smiled as everybody ran

now if I make it through the night, I'll know nothing more
than a vast dark sea

eternity ,
waiting

passing

Tanning grace, dreaming glory
I'm afraid the end is gory.

There's no such thing as Saints
The rot of man is loose

Life's not as nice as yesterday
and it will have to do,

The sunset, it is soiled

Each test is scored with lies

There are no more complete sunrises

Only smokestacks from which to
rise.

3.

California, Land of plenty
I drove my Chevy swift
through the painted pictures of perfection flying high
on hideous insight
Holocaustic nightmares swollen
Concentrating on destruction
dying in the moonlight fine
Staring
in an empty glass of wine,

Eyes closed I have felt
that glow where dreams do dwell
awoken have found wishing wells
dry, but I have held
drifting with the waves
keeping afloat a tune,
flowing with the rhythm of the hour or the moon?

Grown to be a crazy man
   Misunderstood
           today I am, but tomorrow who?
   known to be a hooligan
     worn out engine under the hood
hell bent
   on Resurrection
   Possessed
with mindless good intent
                  Learned to fly
   not to touch the ground
So all these words like large horse droppings settle so uneasy
     as a breeze blows out the smell
              climbing,

drying in the wind and blowing
   nowhere
  flying off too far nobody

     cares

    no one ever saw the sun
      who sailed off too swift
   alienated from all the fun it brought

     no one ever felt the sorrow
  of an easy heart used up and tossed
there were none there to remove the tainted rust

Once I was in heaven
now I'm scaling catwalks
  high above uneven ground
tempted to compete
  Completing the elite
    heartbeat pounding frantically
    I'm romantically inclined
 To surface   somewhere   (anywhere)
soon
        Sun creeps up I cannot hide
       day is calling out again

The rent is due, what sorrow
           where will I go tomorrow?
      Who am I ?   Where am I ?
                 What's to do before I die?
            Can we live and not ask why?
      What is love? And is it
   blind? Kind?
                              hard to find?
   What's worth more
   a dollar or a kiss?
           Earth or a fist?
   A shout or a whisper?

   on a narrow ledge with a tired sigh
   I sleep exhausted with the climb
   Up in the sobering air alone
   Guided by nothing I really know

         Will this mountain all give way?
         Will I know it's peak only in my grave?
         Will I curse myself for climbing?
   At its peak is there

   Love?
         New waves be rolling shortly
            scaring twilight with new dawns

         always are there lessons
   Stairways, but to what?

            after hours wandering
      dreams that seem so bold and new
               get lost in the race without a clue

   If there be fools and geniuses
                        who decides who is who?
            meaning I can mention soon
                  I must conjure

as all rolls on fairweatheredly
  Cold beer while feeding the juke
            memorabilia   gets the blood flowing
        Old times echoing on   and on
                  shadows cast on emptiness

            Bessy lash the little ones with hypnotized eyes
        day and age, let's feel that heartbeat
  Stretches miles of unknown space
                                going down
  Hypnotized by pointless visions
                    vibrating
        Out of control

    Delivered from death back to life I awoke
      to witness
  a babe filled with trivial preconceived dope
      in a city cut off from good soil and soul
    man made desert, architecture in hell
                  my brain spun so coherent I began
          thinking that we could leave the Earth behind
                                to travel
    outward in our mi n d s
                          un til
  a t h o u g h t l e s s   k i s s p o n t a n e o u s embrace
    reminded me
      of mealtime and muzak

        as I strolled unhurried beneath the moon

      tasting the sky
                  smelling the night and watching

  intricate tree branches
              dance .

4.

A foghorn sang all night
Sirens and alleycats wailed their notes
The wisdom of society filled the streets in id pure tones
Pacific wind rattled the windowpane
The unimportant human clock went tick tock
And across the street on the second floor
An Asian girl in a sleeveless dress
Sat playing her piano all night long by candlelight

Her melody so vivid, melancholy and severe
I lit a smoke and hung my head outside to listen
     My table of the elements resting on the floor
Staring at her and she at me
We gazed into eternity
       through sorrow, guilt and ecstacy
               deep

       and I had to ask her,
    Do you feel it to? Feel lost and small?
         Like you've never lived at all?
A burdened artist without praise
   Composing lonely fantasies
              Take
          my hand let's hold
    our heartbeats close
        together and smell
      the morn strange
         see the light change
   I wear a suit and you a dress
    who are we then?
Walking On Shiny Floors
    Squinting In Fluorescent Light
     Ants On A Trojan Sword Into Space
    Swirling
     as we hardly know we're
sailing
     On A Violent Sea
          to a silent   moon ,

I remember
Way back before the dawn began
I was a cloud hung in wonder
          You were a nova waiting to burst
into the sun that spun a galaxy

Then mortal flesh contained us
on Earth we learned of sensual heaven
                    Home for the senses!
          do now we wish to escape again
or are we dependant on
          Earth Air Sea and biology?

          wouldn't we be lonely not knowing the touch?
Wouldn't we be empty without any sense?
          Lost without communication?
               Keep your music playing
          Monkey dance for one more dime
Glancing above these city hovels
               I hear the fatal ticking of time
Stains of evening passed
Pains of bridges burned
Words so cold and dry
Love afar and dying
          While ripe the hour for inspiration
Passing are the sands
     able are my hands
Drums on the horizon beating
     Showdown on the street
One drink at a time, weeping
               Trying to get passed days
that we oughtta be into instead
          Working for chocolate and sweets
While the bread is growing stale
Wondering where tomorrow will linger
Holding on tight to an old serenade
Mistakes are made
     Life washes in cycles
Whirlpools and disgusting tides
          While often forgetting the sum of the sea

We only see what we set out to seek
    Turning the world into a hearse
    Living on only its faults,
Regretting the sun while cursing the clouds
    Hidden inside the brain's hollow vaults
      What occupation is worth more than pleasure?
No treasure shines like the light from within
    Paddling up river, what is the hurry?
      There's but a waterfall sets back the tide
    All night long her music played
with
the foghorns alleycats sirens and wind
 for
the wisdom of society who leaned against
  Locked Doors
and listened.

5.

                  Arise, she said

        So I opened up my eyes
     Your eyes, she said
    are the color of the skies

My eyes, I replied
  Hardly see the light of day
           The day, she mourned
           So quickly runs away.

          Who are we but numbered days
    in pursuit of colored lays?
       Ways which mold us marvelous
Life despite the obvious
      Walking, rocking, talking loud
    Singing in vacant late night streets
Questioning the obvious and blessing the ridiculous
          Fates not yet weakened my young eyes
         Age has not rectified my cries
Eventually will serpents die

and doves fly through immortal skies?

Please play, I said
                    and she ran atop a hill
        Come quick, she played
        and catch me if you will
                    A thrill, I thought
        and I chased her to the top
                    You're up! she cried
        and vanished in the air.

The magic was wonderful
 inspiring and mystical
then came the dawn full of truth,
Morning was practical
 plausible, moral
Frenzied and fatal and lost.

        I saw this vision of a young man with a tie
        Who wasn't stylish struggling to get by
    Who lived and drank too much
        and wasn't happy

            jobs they didn't like
            His friends were bums who didn't have girls,
        they talked about their cars
                            AND DROVE
            ALONE
        to the sunset of oblivion
                            Immortality
with a sharp chord rebellious and free
            Liberation I adore you!
                            Driving dangerous cars swift
        living h i g h in a darkened tunnel
                zig zaggging all through the city awakening
            in the morning with a faint memory
                                of amazement
        that
            blind inside to the World outside
                What is life but a wild ego ride?

I never planned to write these lines
        I never planned
Only dreamt of trophies, not the races that preceded
        Do not aims outweigh anticipated destination?
        Games played, claims made
                happiness profoundly weightless
Time parading
                pleasure masquerading
I know not much of other's tongues
I know I'm not yet in a tomb
I'm drunk and I'm in heaven
        I love this world you lambs!
Weaned on rock'n roll Lived out of control
        Lived fast hard lived lived... . .L   I   V   E
On a dead end speedway
    All us deadhead derelects
                danced on angel dust
                        balancing on rafters high
Vino!~   Vino!   I'll go dry
    Once died a lot for loves that were lost
        once blinded by snowdrifts towards success
        IMAGINATION, How life's enhanced   Whimsically
        in the rain we dance
                        too poor to be charitable
            and too rich to be loved
I am perceptive, I hear an alarm
    Waves crashing on cliffs, wings without Logic
                            dissected
            It's all too much
        Germs
    walls, people and their worlds
Desire overriding sense, emotion overrides desire
            A confident hand for absolute logic
                But what about the infinite?
    the elements exploding
        simple metaphysical
Problems of reality
            The past, does it exist?
                        O future,
    Who are we?

Victims of mortality
Suffering fools capable of breeding
Marching into the streets cocking weapons
Beautiful ideas alive
in our minds
Cocking bayonets unknowing
into the mirror we shoot
and shatter
and the Whole human race goes out with a Bang
Auf wiedersehen mon amour cheerio
La Grande Canal is flowing, parlez-vous
Afternoon is passing, tuck
an educated grip on the reigns steering blind
Who am I to judge mankind?

Walking clear
modern Mountain frontier
escaping   Creating
Reflection   perfection
playing game after game not counting the losses
driving miles an hour through dusk and dawn   To be
Stranded cozily
Reacquainted with humanity
Engine revving smoke polluting forest raping famine neglectors
Growing buds in all directions
embracing, illuminating
Lighting up the Genesis
of fifty-thousand generations
beyond
a flash
of color in the dark
mass against vast emptiness

Can all the masses think so small?
I dream of bees and waterfalls

Cooling the philosophic engines and shifting
to color the shallow cesspool so trivial

In an ardent midnight haze I felt
The weight of the world's ways come bowl
me over beneath the thunder
Ominous clouds moving majestic
Static on the radio expelled music
Trashy words leaped out in blood
the intensity of the moment haunted
I cupped my hands beneath a fountain
but the fire neither stung nor faded.

6.

Forgive me professor for speaking unwise
Earth is my mother, I fear for her life
I bow beneath children and flowers
The whale is my friend
What are we to make of our ways in the end?

Jews in the oven Thousands at a time
Mankind putting mankind in the oven,   Professor
where is the seed
that spawned the weeds that choke the garden?
Is it possible to expel that seed
or has it spread too deep?

Some ancient deep irreversible seed
Is it too late?
as I know we've hardly begun to reach out
into the cosmos surrounding us
as human flatulence wilts so much hope
Look how these flowers could grow
Professor, So much hope
Whithers away
So much potential remains
An educated grip on the reigns steering blind
Is mankind really mad professor?
How crucial is this day in time?

Bells of Christmas guide
filling the unknown
dreaming possibilities
endlessly brought down

Most slammed their doors and they ran
Up the steps right out of the street
Nobody wants to hear those old words
Time not only was the tide
Tim once crowned the smoothest ride
too soon he started looking back
remember thisBOOMremember that?
When was it that his eyes went
pale
recorded love songs then took life
independent grew another mind
as he cried for help to no one,   juxtaposed

On the reckless freeway suicide nothing grows

I seen 'em dead and have buried beloved
poor brother living slow with fast heart attack blood
Dismal chance of hell today
haven't loved in a coon's age
Listening abstracted by the radio
Listening for the tone of an old friend's voice
Listening to much too brilliant abstracts
Shooting arrows in eternity when
the target is nearby

It's not easy to love a sense of humor turned snide
It's heatless upstairs where the fruit is stored
Terrestrial farm had a fresh dead mystery
Grandpa had eggs'n chores and grand
children
How far have I strayed?
Yucky mudcolored dusk
Old midwestern myth toughness revives
Lights inside brighter than the muddy sunset fading

Soon I got me a job that paid pretty well
                Worked nine to five in the city
                Nothing that I did really mattered
                        But it paid well!
                And a mama could a boast a no failure

                                        somewhere must float
                        a relic

                            out in space

            that know one will figure out cause we'll be

gone

Taverns closed

Churches gone

Business done.

7.

murmuring words in comfortable tones
  Left alone
for Twisted humanity, an exit door
  Every being needs a core
     Some cling to never unlocking
Others stray too far to return
          Childhood sought on an intellectual path
            that challenges the world round

  You must go to the mountain
  It's all that's left to do
    Friends will keep you warm there
  as only friends can do

     Christian bells afrost
         fearing the unknown
           Dreaming past abilities
Never let you down.

      Each but a fraction of a larger crowd
Nothing lasts that long, disposable
 Water skis to walk on water, Who
has a brain?
     Those who follow or question everything?

   Are the unconventional more sane
    than an audience in fear of making mistakes?

The Daily News paints twisted pictures
    truth cannot diminish
  so far out on a limb little noticed.

8.

Only booze can save you now
(Stop making decisions
delve into
theacid p o o ; l

Heavy sea, Endlessl ykn ocking
Out of the cradleceaseless ly mocking   )

Poets by the sea come forth
Shall we stand
Walk hand in hand?
What does it take to make a show felt?
To circulate questioning eyes
I lie and dream and die and rise
Laughing with madmen, ignorant wise
noble, powerful, corruptible and love-able
Getting physical, intellectual, emotional and   common
running round the edges of a picture frame
Half sane
merry despite the thunder calling
Before dawn the fire, so faint and neglected
after the sunset, Brilliant with awe
rUSHING
Out of basement bistros bars and coffeehouses
Something wild aFLIGHT aFAR

After the steam breath, crisp mountain morning
Sober or intoxicated, is that the real question?

Look at the gray smog over the sunset
aloof in L.A.'s generic gloss
Look at the things that make you laugh
the Masks
is any of it real at all?
Smiling, smiling
idiot smile
Calm down and be cool fool
staring out a windowpane
Enclosed inside a glass egg rising Up atop some mountain

Waiting for this egg to crack
    waiting to hatch in to stone,
        Nobody lives that long, disposable
Nobody's in control! replaceable
do I have to ask myself?   Why must I wonder
Must I stumble so to learn ?   must I feel the thunder?

        Come in tune oh outward one
            or what's your vision?

do you shit out mangled Bongos
            Or hit upon a chord?

            Banish those foolish ideals and see
Violent nature, Poignant, purposeless
        Until MAN came
                    along to clarify conquer and tame
            the cosmos for better
        for worse for
        our own purpose
                Seizing eternity, the Deadly Atom!
Foolish? brilliant?   alas who's greater?
        Politics to organize,   science to explore
            Culture to refine
    The farsighted and the blind,
                            Leading
                the warm and kind bestowing
            Narrow hearts and brains destroying
    No empty void
    No walls
Just human perception loving   grocery   lists
    trends life and reality brewing
        Unearthed coral
            antique outlooks
            Nightmare monstrosities
            aiming while we shoot too high
    Airplanes dropping bombs from the sky
                        neglected while we all get high
    on
        suicide.

Symphonies of reckless lives out of control
Madness worshipped, elected into office
Reflects across the world
acid Rain on the windowpane
Insane pledges overdoses
numbed dying out by the television
Frying in the microwave, an accident that glows

We rose playing with the fire
Political, analytical, philosophically contagious
Rattling cages of contentment
Shouting curses of catastrophe
Nearsighted, loudmouthed, proud and suicidal
How did we get here?
Good-bye lame ducks, good-bye ma
Off we go to holocaustic sunsets
While our minds fade off to some hollow destination
Aloof all old principles seem to fade
as here we are dancing in a place we'd never dreamed
where animals proceed to
growl
Now give me whiskey and wild passion
Balancing on rafters high
Clear horizon high above this city maze dead end as
the streets are rushing round in circles
mutants! Mutants!
praising culture
pock marked elephants deformed in fashion eating
food derived synthetically ate on the run

Half the sockets missing bulbs
Grist to the mill, anchors aweigh!
Visions of texture existing
among mysteries to be sailed
through like a continuous flow
Rich with highs, deep with lows
continuous slopes
falling waters
Earth's intelligence reckoning
creatures thought divine

Out there lies
    the great unknown
  as inward lies
      a rolling stone
          On what plane lies this humble day?
       The times are mad I read today!
    pleasant dreams to your children
        Don't try to question why
         Be a fool and you'll fly
   Love is kind, until the day
        when it runs away, it tears
      Takes so long to repair, your eyes
    Cut right through a hundred disguises
     It may be a disease, so what
     I've caught it, you've caught it
        Let's both go
    Blind

Cold the sand, sane the stride

Pacified by a bottle of wine

Open eyes, ears, mind and fly
Embarrassments are kind
Rattling the cage

Intrigue sets the stage

pages of my mind are turned
the sublime blurred

we'll lie in a casket, we'll sleep in the ground
alas
what've we to be proud of but dawn?

9.

Cooling the philosophic engines and shifting
      to color the shallow cesspool so trivial

                    reaching up to absorb

   realization

 of pure sensual pleasure

     waves crashing on cliffs, wings without logic

Sad, dramatic hours of ecstacy
      guide boats across an infinite sea

      through dead eyed sophistication
                           inspiring
  to run Beyond

the routine dawn

    to see beyond mountains and time, to see clearly
    The complexity, beauty and mystery of being

   existing
        amidst
              humbling
d

   e

      p

         t

           h

wondrous enormity, I never dreamt
of all life's turns

such mystery, marvel, joy and sorrow

Weaving in and out grand chords

Vastly different footsteps on the stairway into
        some eyes scared, some curious, closed

begging for meanings behind symbols
        This tragic reality needn't be sad, please
keep the air clean
        and calm enough to dream
                effectively,

                Time, space and the universe
        Drives by itself
                        forever and ever

mind

                a bud

                Blossoming unto beyond

        a tiny island,

    isolated

        quaking

10.

softly
  come tender
Let our strength be known
 Let all our power unleash beauty and hope
   this be my prayer as I lye down to sleep
      dreaming of the bud before the bang

hoping my routine lends a hand
                  in
                      the flowering
      of understanding

  They came hunting, I went weeping
     The machine was turning and I was a screw loose
    Hiding in the woods spewing out unsteady visions
   Watching with bad breath the madness
 Forgetting horror, but we can't
 Once we kissed
   In the backseat, on the lawn
On the cold roof as snow fell
Crazy characters dancing through dawn
        Darkened by the brightness gone
           all falls
         We flow
       beyond death
     who knows?
    Simple minds
     Talking heads
  Frigid bed   Curtain call
Freaks of creativity howl
  Open city Open mind
   Sinking drop by drop in the sea

eternity,

Weak minds feed the fever
Sharp minds feel the blood
Trampling clover, soon its over
In the field lies a dove.

Fleas Inside the Store

1

What is in the night sky

amputated

migrating to

where love and pity

lie entombed

wld gh sht

frw   quy   vxy trz

dim dim mim ssftii fffeee

2

why must you justify
               your existence by baking a cherry pie?
               why contemplate til the day is lost?
          crushed by your impenetrable thought universe
               when will you retire, when
               will you hear the leaves rustle
               chipmunks chatter
          climbing ladders, stepping up
               to that step that says not a step
          slip and break your back lying
               in the garden, rose thorns in your flesh
          soil on your palms, paint on your face
               lying in the garden not getting up
          no calls for help, no quick comeback no
               will to block this reflection.

3

Impatient, I lye
    in a weed patch beneath
    a neglected sky, my heaven

no higher than footsteps
    in the passing sand

    a child's land

               fantastic feeding
    as science drives

    outward delivering

Stirring still waters to see passed a mirror.

4

3:09 and I must run
To catch the plane I'm flying on
Somewhere through unheated cities
Somewhere to a strange rainbow
I must go
Shower shave and leap to life
Tie straitened, smile painted
And when I get home I'll barf it all
up

When I get home
I'll eat before I sleep
I'll think I'll have a beer or ten
Then forward will I go
To paint some pointless show
When I awake my head will hurt

3:14 and I must run
Senseless but I need the money
Apathetic but I got the job
Breathless without purpose is hell
Hell Hell Hell hell Hell! Hell! Hell!

5

There was something sort of tragic in his eyes
The way Will Robinson disguised his lies,
Smiling as if to cover up some endless tragedy
And ain't that just the way to be
I freak for you, you freak for me
And what a bundle of conformity we can be
Put pot roasts in the oven
Buy happiness on sale
Put humanity in the oven
There's no value today

Come morn there'll be
Heaven
Like yesteryear, its off today
Out golfing by the lake and lounging
Cooled by an electric air conditioner

Purr kittens raised on thick shag carpet
Purr in mittens never questioned
The way Will Robinson disguised
There was a lost look in his eyes
Hypnotic, withdrawn, brain afar
Given to disappearing, icy strings
A happy place, but empty space
And ain't that just the way to be?

6

So diligently dying
Magnificently dreaming
What brilliant inconsistency
The art of alien age

New directions? Old ways
Thoroughly astute ideals
Aflight in mind, afar from
a cold, weathered bed

So diligently dying
If not for flesh for art
In search of true redemption
by contrivance, life eclipsed.

7

Telephone ringing
Hop out of bed
Morning is messy
Will the day drowned?

Hole in my sport coat
Growl in my belly
Off to the cafe
To write of the smell

Part of it pretty
A lot of it flat
Stirring and sipping
In search of good taste

Immune to distraction
Blind like a pig
Clocks race too quick
Then off I go dancing
Scribbling spirit possessed

Where did it come from?
Thank God it's all down
Soon leisure runs thin
Plotting out the next step

Falling weary in bed contemplative
Listening to the last extraneous sounds
Balancing the lost and found on a scale
All forgotten by the next morning's dawn.

8

Anywhere
Makes no difference
Huddle with me by the autoware
I'm a creature just like you
Let's do what living creatures do

gootchie goo little young one snuggled
In the sheltered nest
Luckier than the rest
Cynical and guilty as
Hell with a conscious
Admitfully void
of Awareness and Bliss

Relief from labor   Weekend for two
To stroll through moistened streets
Reflecting the lamplight
Asleep against the dew, hearing crickets chirp

Watching surveyors
Stoned on a hill
Give a tour to their students

feeling the wind blow
Saluting the day
 passing
questioning cohesivity
graphability

Conclusive respectability

is
Science fiction

Sorry Bean
King of your dream

9

Life is short

When you die
Who gives a snort
Modern Rome
Louder! Louder!
Wealthy throne, worldly black hole
Black and white stereotypes
Cosmic creatures trying on cartoons
Party hardy every body party hearty

Pure delicious raucous spirit
Invades a white suburban home
Clean kept middle conformity
Harassed by vulgar energy
Soul rhythms, honest curses
           Sounds from the heart
                      Feedback and screams
              Protests about pathetic news
        That pop don't wanna hear
     And ma don't wanna see
As sweet sixteen outgrows her party dress
   and the pride of the class becomes a freak
Looking back most teachers were
      Shepherds with their backs to the unknown
   While poets of the airwaves hold
                 their weight year after Year

A conspiracle connection, winding
      Up a swift machine pumping blood
        Underlying culture, heart attack producer
Faster! Louder!
       Faster Hyper
             active conscious
         REBEL BEFORE APPRECIATION
            Destroy the hometies!
     Destroy windchimes!
Drowned it all out
eat the pie.

10

Speak little Nilly weeping
To the dirt and sky
 and Peoplemoving shadows stacked
Monster marvelous machines
Rapid 20th century   Begotten
Oh?
       Little Nilly cursing
                Ho!
       Little Nilly hanging
               It

                                    up
 dissolving Littly Nil searching
for a profound kiss
 into bliss
If
dirt and sand grow flowers
A then B, biology
dissecting Squeamish heart surgery
               Blood drops
       Philosophy
                 Rapid 20th Century
    Earth mmmovers, satellite antenna eyes
         Ears and robot mind
                 Little Nilly
        Clapping at ancient lines
     Nature unkind
     Wind
Littly Nil
      That out of date clock and catch
          The eight-forty-three, Get
    out of those baby blue colors and get
Yourself a suit and tie to work for
    Plastic Apprehension - Polyester Necessity
Speak Little Nilly Nil, speak to the cows
      Grazing

11

Beauty here, beauty there
　　　Beauty everywhere
　　Beauty found in bluejeans
　　　Beauty in the backseat
　　　　　　　　　　　　　Heed
　　　　　　　　The calling of a foul deed

Beauty in each twilight, beauty in the bar
Beauty moving precious in the backseat of the car

　　　　　　　　　　　　　Yesterday
　　　　　　　　A madhouse worshipped
　　　　　　　　　　Today
　　　　　　　A rainy painting lost
Young will soon get old
　　　and old look to the young
Beauty in a whisper, beauty in the lungs

　　　　　　Surreal
　　　　　　　　The talent of the mind
　　　A mime
　　　　　　Is playing in my heart
　　A blessing
　　　　　Perhaps best be restored
　　　　　　　　　　　　　　　Or
　　　　　　　　Anything might happen

　　Blindness led to sight
　　　Forgiving
　　Precious thought abrupt
　　　Delivering
　　Wasted away moments
　　　　Mourning
　　　Stormed atop a cliff
　　　　　　Chasing

Lame   Tame

Wild

Insane

A crazy haze
Fills the maze
Orderly days are sunk
The kitchen sink is clogged

Working like a dog

Despicable
Eating like a hog
In gluttony
Carousing like a drunk
Perpetually
Nothing goes as planned

Hand   Head
Work   Play
Today in flames
Growing pains
Grabbing the reigns and running

Wild

Leading parades of honest

Promise

Colors and fashion replaced
Leaping impossible boundaries
Risen up from kitchen scraps
Age old beauty
Sailing on a melody
To and fro, flowing
Like a river without knowing.

12

Travelers alone
Nobly pursuing
Without a reality

Afar from the touch
Of reaction and crutch

The direction of history
Proceeds
On a theoretical-proof existence

One can never predict
And there is no substitute
For the strange

Ungraphable waves
Of emotion

13

Poignant apprehension
Of quintessential
                          subtlety
Bulldozed by mechanical
Programming

          myriad of confusion

What shall I do today?
Watch the trees sway?
Study or play? Paint on a white
 canvas a vision?

Swashbuckler delusion

Romantic Heaven, no
                                    Uniformity

          Transition
          From sword to flower

                                    Delinquent

                    while

          The spirit soars!

14

Don't the thistles make you curious?

                Turtles in the road?   and saints?

     Battlescars from a B-grade

             Heavy vessels to our   legends

                       Lunar stockings

*   here can we be

             Where do we put the cartoon elevator noise?

There's a noose hanging down from the moon

          There's a policeman wagging a devil's tail

  I saw God giving up,   retreating to the other side

Bright Northern Duskburn your eye

                   Don't stare at the sun fool!

          Some twisted sisters came to advertise

       Ambitious young champion of the Market

   Ran out of ham on Christmas Eve

Whiskey was free, we drank to the kid

Dressed in gum wrappers, paper napkin eyes

                Friends from the sitcoms

              Every one had anecdotes

     Good dope Behind our back

  Smoked humor, tits and totties

 Robbed the cradle, Beat the wife

 Bought off the farmer resolved the strike

Bootstraps and collars

     No nakedness taking a pose for the history books

REverse the conscious and the un

Computer cosmic politician

Steely Dan

Bring me down to the ground, I

don't wanna fly

the endless sky forever

Lots of expansion to bare

All the here and there to transpose.

15

Moving into outer space
These mortal hands
Create
Neon sundown, nuclear ghost
These hands that hold you
Fight and bleed
Eerie chants, electricity
Heartbeat breath
These hands quiver   Society snoring
                                           Casual
                    Expressionless waste conventionality
                              Head sharp beyond life
                    Feedback for sheep, grass for elite
                    Spirit waking in body lifting
                    Monotone news
                    Conversation awaiting intoxication:
                                              Priceless
                    Eyeballs   Pearls   Brains   Rust
            Hold on hold out
                    A microchip heart have you?
Computer logic?   Selfish lies?
            Cry souls in question
                              Mocked by the blind
        Spirit contained physical strain
                              Practical nowhere reigning
                    No soul. No love. Confusion.
            Noise.   Junk.

Fixations on
ideals   Mistakes
                              Rhythms
            Desire
                                                            Neglected change

                                                            Moldings patterns

                                                            Impressionistic apparel

Purity
  Corrupting vision
      Emotion
  Adding grace
        Mystic meddling
Visiting nearsight
      Thinking photos
      Talking heads

        Lifebeat
        Arousing

        Children tending
        Crowds shouting curses

Sweat beneath my smile
Touch this trembling hand
Stains on my overcoat
Dust blows through my veins
Haunting melodies play
Smoke on the horizon
Bribes to bake the heart
Glitter please the glossy
Spikes piercing ambition
Modern day
Hell and heaven
Neighbors on Earth
hell and Heaven
Recognizing symbols of hope and despair
Never retreating
Children of prosperous
Earth tending
Decaying mother without spirit
The future is not in your mind
Your mind is filled with your own life
Stains beneath my sweating smile
Me and you are dying
And this interview doesn't matter sir
My qualifications mean nothing
My resume is pointless
Your business here is unimportant.

16

Are we all dreaming?
The rest just wants to slide down hill

I stick my tongue out on my words and burn my eyes yes on the
nobody says nothing but keep the lid on tight
everybody feels they need a job
and so do I but where am I
Beebopping blinded by
Guilt

Ah poetry, although I'm sick of sappy odes

Say I really wanna live awhile, I said it before
But the meaning keeps changing while
The worlds expectations rearrange
Or has it always been the same
kinda game
Just getting full of wires now?

Lapped onto the most beautiful concept ever dreamed
For what?

This is no change
Just work like a maddog
Everything youthink is bothering
It'd be nice to really love a picnic
I'm going blind
Deaf and dumb
Out in the wilderness even.

17

Friends bring me books

As I swing on a vine
From media to my sharpest eye
ear and tongue:
        Media

Images images
        Hypnotic
Why dig for content?
    apart from machin e
Mind propelled
        Heart Unto eternity
    Why whisper in the dark?

Transport me to a horizon simple
A barren desert, no more than two
        solid colors
To counter balance a collage of detailed information
cluttered wires in the brain
Blindly let me smell and touch another naked being
Let me smell and feel their breath
and they mine
Let me diagram them in my own mind
and they me
Then lets exchange secret
thoughts unspoken.

18

If
Then sailors
(Pirate material if so led)
tend the sheep of sheer indulgence
                              Then
                                    Carried away by metaphor
            Valor
      Must be something in the soul.

                  Oh joy discovery
                                          do I fear i'll break you?
                        oh spirit screen
do you think we'll go far?
                                          oh ancient dream
            was is it we're here for?

                                    angle on a wing angel dream
actress of ouji
                        macho huff

SharpedgeTerror
BassDrumFreaks
headmasterbaterforgloriousthings
                              Shine your weary eyes
            Survive through the night
You can tint the screen
   Beam it up bright or down low
            Shine your perpetual change   on   to   heaven
      Cosmic travellors dropped in

            It won't be long the hand is strong
            Minds offtune
            We the abused
                              Children consumers
                  Who knows where?
                        Stroking hair
Stoned little mary always at home
            REciever answer your telephone

Sirens race the street
                              devoid and sheik
                Constipated lolly pops trotting
        Ambivalent how'r ya's
Engine turning
               Predicate binds
               Skidding tire death is
                        what is
real.   .   .   .
and in time sterile mannequin clones court the record machine
                        Barbie dolls begin to dream
        Dimestore Pilgrims Rise to Greatness
                            Her breast is numb, bum
               Get outta my hair
You're not gettin anywhere   birdsing high inthetrees
                        Acrobat leaves, afloat
                   Trite punctuation hurts
          Angular seas marijuana
                 Heaven lost in seven-eleven
        the crash half as bad as it seems
              wish this day would last forever
By what means motivate?
                 work brings you down
Swift strokes on the rich course ain't worth a thing
           marbles and pins
      Soda fountain with a wind up
    telephone
           Got run over by a car too far dreamer
    clouds   drifting ajar
                 Guitar Joe Snorts
       a   Traditional Street
              filled with treats
n Got run over by a car
               Sevenfourtyseven flying
       Late ripe wintersun
Soon a Northern Dawn, a whole new language
                   Sentimental
    Target for disaster way too high

                                          hillbillyboisenberry
          Smiling
                              witha capital s
    nuclear undergroundacid rain
              Those near the bay pay
                        outrageous guessing games
    Sloppy celibate bum on a holiday
                          Shouts for fictional hooligans

          The rainbow over disneyland smiles

                        19

    A breeze bangs the shutters
              and bangs the shutter
              and bangs the
                          shutters

                        Have memory on this dinosaur
                        I caught a glimpse but it got away
                        Tomorrow is a speeding plane
                        Tonight the nigger gets revenge
                        Tomorrow a new underdog begins,

        At the laundromat I suffer dryer tumble vertigo
              As the shutters bang
                    and a woman asks
                        Who care's where we're going?
        Who care's where we've been?
                                    we part as we began
                    Superman's on vacation
          Gimme a countdown and relay back r e g g a e

    Ka-Boom!

20

Bing bang
Macho Achoo
Gotcha!

Ang Lang
Aud Seine
Dant Bled
Brrr...

Ripe Pipe
Love Dike
Flood Thumb
Whoah!

Gone gone
Loss Strong
Wash Hog
Flogged

21

Strangely staring
Out from the front page
Into the television screen
Avoiding my gaze
Elusive and vague
A world that escapes
Your heroin dark eyes
Look out and see what you reflect
A sincere mystery, Aren't we all a judge?
                    Or
Is it just a pose for the camera
Text for purpose
Flowing tide
Strapped in techno roller coaster
Bulldozing ozone
            Screaming excitement
Death near is ripe.

Breath my pipe
Stop the dike
Calling home
A bed to warm
Precious waste
Ruffled lace
Million race
A billion souls
  Suspicious
          Touch
Mango   Kiwi
        Slide rule   Pygmy
Chinese   laundry
      Propagate
                              Fate
                  Laugh
                                      Magazine
                    I
            want
      to   forever

22

Cocaine, quaaludes, overdose
Comatose
Culture in excess
Luxuries now necessities
Beers counteract the coffee
Coffee counteracts the beer
Child cries for
     more more more
products learned on tele v
        I want want want
   No end in sight
but someday America promises
More sleep with greater heat
More varieties of shoes to decorate
feet More
Sales pitches, credit extended
MORE
unused junk for the Christmas tree
THREE
hundred billion dollars of bombs
   Enough to feed
    the world but no!
   Bug spray to zap ants on the window
   Sterilize ! forget dirt
    conceal it
    among a universe considerably empty
   And why bewilderment with mourning?

   Shadows peeking over cobwebs wet with dew
     Teeth stained with residue
   Tommy gunz eclipsing
     Glorious, Notorious
          Truth heartless turtle
        None but a shell
Speak inspiration fella
Or take your place on the chain gang

Have you smelled the air lately?
It makes the movies all so real

Dogs in the cafeteria seeking
Table scraps and affection

Crickets in the evening countryside
chirping

Moon up, fire down
It's easy to forget the chaos of humanity

The most crucial of arts does not last

To cut and paste a superior collage requires
Knowledge of the last crumb on the floor
Acknowledging the sticky ketchup bottle
Beer stained napkins
Metaphors of culture
unrealized
Showered with reprise
Toward the end
of the twentieth century

on a beautiful, forgettable Sunday.

23

Goof

        Silly goose
        Caboose
            Waddling
        Quack! Quack! Quack!
        On still waters   Miniature might
                    Delight
                    Artificial elegance
                Intelligence
                  It's all happening
                    Yeah yeah yeah
              I don't know why I just
        Time   do
     Table vibrating
  Colored maps on the wall
        Down the hall
Fog

             Smoke
    Bellicose diligence
Six pence   Creep
      Creed
              Halo
       Ha-ha-ha!
              Ecstacy and flesh
   Bashful busybodies
        Out of date jalopies
              Naughty
      Sin sin sin sins
        Let me in let
        The light in open
     The big doors to
              Ah-ha-ha-ha
       Enchantment, wonderland
Green isle of Alice
             Simple tent pitch city
      Witty
        Earthy
          naked

24

Sea-drops
Thistles full of missiles
Why not missile-toes instead?
Nose to sulfur
Doom explode
Atomic missiles
Forward with the art race!
Forget the insane arm's race
The times are **MAD MAD MAD**
As man has ever been
Woman lead us in
Demons foul breath
Venom spew sperm sells
Putrid gobbly-gook
Are we living yet?
Outrageousness to combat
Zany ludicrousity, I've teardrops
Worthless in a sea so vast.

25

Follow the line on the floor beep
Silence in a dustless
Immaculate conception

Institutions got me
I can't go outside
Institutions got me
And I'm high inside
In the future maybe
I'll break out and maybe
I'll be a child
                    Maybe
A ranting raving destined
Man
Institutions got me
and I'm forming

Follow the line on the floor beep
Silence in a dustless
Immaculate conception

26

departing now

Nine o'clock
Time to stop
Fidgeting bam bam
Another scam to impress the man
Another weep to court the meek
Gee but it's sweet to sleep
In a lullaby elite
But I must make my ode
And prayer to you
Raspy old fool still dreaming
Of life beyond rainbows, a place
for us.

27

I was determined to borrow some scissors and call off the National Guard when in came the bow-tie man and told me that I should feed the unicorns before the snow starts flying in May and before those good 'ol boys from Babylon start racing their turtles on Capital Hill and calling the Andersons to ask them if they would like to come over for punch and cookies after they saw the movie about filth and perversion in the city of brotherly love where a universal understanding of the fact that anteaters don't eat planets because marionettes can't survive without their strings and even if they could run amok across topographical maps it would be pointless since lunch is served at noon and after that they could always run over to Suzan's house and play with the computer until her mother stumbled in and threw out all the children of the rich because they were asking for trouble by poking grandma's eyes out and smashing ants into the television screen just when John Wayne was starring in The Alamo one Sunday afternoon the rain was pouring down like boysenberries from Bolivian Belle's bowling ball that bore a beautiful inscription saying something about how slaves with painted faces never played in Pandora's sandbox because the king went stir crazy over his lusty wife that cheated him out of all his riches and sent some mumbling moccasins from Mozambique to the Isle of Gilligan with Louisiana Whiskey and the children of the man that helped shape our minds by showing us that we are more than just a bunch of babbling idiots who think that life is nothing more than a second of seven minutes in heaven.

28

The problem Is
That I'm too
STONED
To sing to pygmies

Afternoon in my room
Held hostage by the muse
This is where the light is best
Let's see what the grand piano plays us

Nothing, Did I blow the trip?
Speeding through, you fool
Are you full?

Lightning forms a Greek cafe
Misfortune in Corfu

Margo like's this give up music
Shallow as the day is long
It echoes down the embassy hall
To my padded cell
The wishing well
Where all's as white as nightmare fright
Looking sharp
 Hiding falls
        life is bold
Clap your hands for prophets in a rock band
Let the music fade the news
Riding the muse, hunting daydreams
As afternoon fog rolls
over the Western Addition
                    I'll build you a castle for us to share.

29

What strange rhythm
Is it at all connected?
Can I dive in and return whole?
Hasn't it all been done before?

Spread out strangely
Used up hours, edited
into literature, to be consumed
by those who fear
Living
Is swinging
overhead waiting
For the human song to cease
Where in these days am I?
What's said and what's
the connection
to dreams between scenes seems I'm not
paying attention On auto pilot in
a thoughtless world more a machine than a human being losing
Touch with its more visionary
Side   Bang Boom Salvo
Fog rolling into the photograph
Toes like harnessed beasts rebel
A foghorn blows out of context
Clock ticks collapses
The heat the Heat
wishing the well
Where
Is the honest white line
That marks the boundaries
Of heaven
And how long
Before this hellish void
Collapses
And who's responsible
For sorrow and bliss
If not the composer of
These windows?

30

Mars scars
Put your hat on
Please grease the
Pied pooper
Pilgrimming unto
Adieu

True to vivid colors cosmos vowels
Venom verbs off Dover cliffs
Irish stale beer smoke smelling love pub
Psychedelia San Frantabulation
        Automation
Mars scars
Spin the ferris wheel
Venereal surreality between
Sheets of sweeping
Subtle teasing
Goo-day misses May
Wanna play whiff my persona?
Bergman stretched the big scream
Lingering outside an ice cream parlour

Mars scars
Put your hat on please
Tease the windshield wiper
One more time adding value to dimes
Away in a vault, proud walk
Away
On a mind's planet far from the plane
Through a dirty windowpane.

31

Livin on babies
Under sedation
That's the way it goes   I'm no
                                    Critic of the circus
                                                          But
            Maybe you'd like your picture taken?

What about love? Whataboutit?
What about
The Alamo and Custer?
Destiny manifested as a great frontier
I could grow to love you
Or I could grow to kill

Let her ease, please the pleased
Release the haze
Purple trim
Baby blue submarine parked off the lawn
But the plot don't get along fast enough
And those near don't really reach far
                    Enough
And the brass section's louder than
            the wind section, but I'm
So glad you made it

Welcome to fantasyland

Hazy from the smoke
Why do you think they call it dope?
Band-aid box and tie-dyed banner
Running low on batteries,

Confidence level alternating
Peek-a-boo reality
Psuedo-
Dreams

Free from the medium
Pee for the press
That's the secret to success
But windows are a great thing, really

Knock-knock, anyone home inside?
Mars is in retrograde, the sun doesn't set
Round the clock possessed

It's hardest to say good-bye
To the last who bought the bullshit
Hot ashes waving proud
Can you paint the room a little brighter?
Make art of the ruins?
M-Maybe do something incredible
Like warm a barstool@#$%^&*|}{?:"><)*&-+=~,

".":....:
          :....:   #*^*#
             :....":'^~~~   ~~~~~~^':".......:

\\\\\\\\\||//////////\\//\\/\/\/\/\/\/\/\/\/\//\\
///\/\/\/\\/\/\/\/]}}{{}{}{[\\=\\//><><><><><><><=
==||===~~~~^<>|||/\/\/\///\\\
                 WW#$FX@&H&?K

AA$$!@@**^^)(^^**@@!$$BB

         LLULIUOYGQYTPIFUQWCVGMJSDUERTPPIUORT
?

32

Digging a hole in the road
To find what's underneath
Deep as all hell I see
In the pit looking up at the sky

Shrugging my motions to climb back up
Kissing the pavement when back on the road
Travelling, then digging all over again.

33

circles

                circles

     light   and dark

          daytime is

       no

    TROUBLE

       things of the water

          things of the air

   a tree bleeds

----
in the rear view mirror of a truck we see
belief
in masks

evidence
of things unseen

34

I been up all night inspired
Let me lay this down for you
just the way I wanna do
Success is dirt
For gardens
beneath a fresh fog ceiling propelled
Beyond news to the
eternities
Whole
outer space, to the great unknown
Out of the cradle endlessly reaching
cosmic mind petty toll
I feel the globe as home, sweet
Teacher elevate
over image
Titles
Plotless glossy
Deceitful propaganda
Lies to bed a lover down
Then off goes the rat on another journey
From the West Coast to the East
Through
undiscovered poetry
Unsung hell and sterile highway
Through zombie towns
of humanity
squeezing like a sponge and tasting blood
Pick my brain apart like birds with beaks eat crumbs
Listen to nature
human's extension
January twenty-eighth nineteen hundred and eighty six
BOOM!
Half a mile up in the sky
Blows the Challenger
no survive
Stretching reaching
human trials the
risks, price to pay
strangeness numbness vagueness

Through rich enchanted lands, America
Undisclosed
 diversity unflowing, undiscovered
 truth fed and put to sleep by media
I smell
Sweat beneath the make-up reading bathroom stalls

Machine or human being?
Above individual thoughts
Collective all
possess their noble rot
And I'm inclined to hunger.

35

Poison drink we

To bring glee
Pleasure poison
Poison treasure
Drink we poison
Kills the brain
Destroys the sane
Relieves the rain, they say
Drunk every day is
Poison poison
Why?

Distorts vision drastically
Affects the days tranquility
Leads to much regretted deeds
Dead drunk in the toilet
Dead wreck on the road
Dead from drinking poison
Favorite vice

Nice and sociable
Poison parties
Poison promise
Poison poison
With your lunch
      Poison centers
      Poison temples
      Religious poison
      Poison poison
      Kills the body kill the mind
      Bottles of poison
      Bottles elite
      Poisoned fellas sleep in the street
Poisoned fellas can't stand on their feet
Poison leads to poison
    Leads to poison
    Leads to
Hell ringer
Head banger
Strange manger
      Rearranged
      Danger! Danger
      Veiled in black
      Cometh the stranger
      Dusting the track with
Poison
      Busting the statue of
Reason --   Poison
      Rusting the realm of the
          Senses, substance
      Smoldering ashes remain
The poison
      Stranger respects his
Poison poison
High

36

Budweiser
Bullion
Wasto alienation
Morphine Oompah
Ghoulish slaves
Baby cakes
In crib dreams
Schem
ing

No sight
Fire
Hearth spoiling
Oil rigged
Big on digging
Dated crazes
Missing pages
Fearing insanity

At last
Sweet music shines through suicide
Impossible bliss circling
Ashes
Of intoxicated spring

Seriously
Spinning webs
Good-bye forever
Big pillar
Catch ya never
Scratched skin surface
Heavy blood
Wouldn't join the worship
A moment's reflection
Compartmentalized

Aaaaaahhhhh

Ooooohhhh

Weather vane

Don't wanna be a poet
Wanna be
A normal fool
Misunderstood
Dogs in the wood
Bleary eyed in the sticks
Keen on mirage
In tune to the fix

'ts all out of hand
Beyond command
Forget the art
Of dilemma for spark
Preparing the ark
Political fools
Deserve a big hand

Black and white
Fall
In favor of the furor or
Go forth unchartered

God sent a pill
To scramble the world
To end all this climbing
He didn't make it easy

Immune to the thrill
It all led to fighting
Getting groomed in the mirror
Reality cracked

Will ever I be free?
From philosophic bonding
Whatever works
To get by
Til I die

Simple melodrama
Collapses
Beneath a solid sense
Of senselessness

Machismo chains
Known insane
Addicting, just the same

37

In the midday sun
A man beat up a flower
To teach a bird a lesson
He laughed a wicked laugh of death.

38

Young child
Laughing pure
Adoring
A world whole
That the old man
Lost

Time plays tricks
Loses battles
Women on sailboats in summer
Dreams
Forever more intriguing
Than

Child yawns, weary bones
Time left to bounce
Receiving
Gave an ounce
Alive accept
The way things are
See beauty bloom
Amidst the boat without
Rocking

Alleycats croon
Old transient moon
I have crossed deserts and
mountains and Grown
and nothing makes more sense
Than nonsense

Angry storm
Full of scorn
Misfit
Erase my knowledge
Praise
Happiness

Rush hour traffic
Hot smelly smog
Clerk watches her clock
Among this crime and decadence
Is this where modern
Culture is?

Feeble ambitions grand
In everybodies head
Unique characters on the street
Don't scribble that rusty heart
In the ground

Hot summer
Night begins
Versatile
And poor
Adoring drained bewilderment
More flesh and soul!   Cuban cigar
More flesh and soul!   Dingy hotel room
                                          Trivial newsprint
                            There goes the world.

39

days
        drift away
without a monument

but life is not a field of headstones
it is one

40

Oh damned up fury
With all my heart
I pore my art, a substitute
For love into the stew
Of consciousness, a life created
In hope's of life, unalienated

Where lingers inner and outer peace?
Elevated from need, void of redemption
Souls dry in societal molds
Or do
They really come clean, unbroken?

Do mirages magnify truth?
With all the damned up
Fury I thrust my sharpened pen, my sword
Into the mind of the partly recoiled
A warrior
Impolite
impatient, no satisfaction.

42

moneymoneymoneymoneymoneymoneymoneymoneymoney
if you wanna cut the world apart don't come to me
numnuts eating christmas trees
beggars banking   my guru says
                              make inner space cosmic
                        skate on the ice rink of your dreams
don't groove on fairy tale impostors
grabbing control of
destiny
i like my coffee black

make sure you know when you're high
just when you thought you died
the world is getting deeper
hyper-motive
blaspheme creampuffs
                              phooey   wamblast
                  take your rodgheruzi
dam blast
ram shitty shilhead harbour tuba town trumpet
                                    we're going round the clock
                                        this time
                                        it's kiss time
                        no more pretending
                        we don't drink lukewarm coffee
            nor nothing sugar free   old rock'n roll dreams
quit shittin sentiment on the pot
                  it's wee wee hour
                  it's long been dark
            nod if you can hear me. hiding
                        in the shadow of a page
swinging
                                    an axe upon a dead tree
                                        in the forest
                        proud
            cool wind against your ego sweat
                                        steadfast
I open my arms.

43

Once I separated the man from the   myth
And got over the all consuming nothingness s
Living is art, hearts   are   immune
Harmony   blooms from a   love less   ruin
While our minds are in tune
And the   mandolin   plays
To a conspicuous season's

    question of time and deadline
    A few innocent words don't compute
    Relevant find one harassment
    Multiplies by a million and two

        Strange how the cosmos got small
        By the river flowing gasoline rainbows
        Where the milkman mixed his brew
        And spilled a few, The shit
        goes down the drain
        Away from the brain.

44

Once, in a while
Dawn's magnificent
Colors sharply
Balance
Bottles crashing on pavement
      Siren's a wail
Once, for a while
Density forms
Destiny norms
Moments expand
Punctuated
      Frightened
Brainy skeletons and skin
Hairdryer plugged
In
Fracturing ethics diseased heart
Warping
Musical grooves
Moving pictures on walls
Illuminating darkness
Cerebellum smoke
Makeshift reality
Factory food
While in a once
Episodic recall
A jar full of matchbooks from bars and places
Essential priority
Music box musty heaven
Maniac dreams and idiot lines
                     Tenderly spoken
           Lovingly

             longingly,

45

Sorrowful soldiers of temper and myth
Maybe this shipwreck is nothing new
Sometimes a neighbor has offered

A media revelation, a sleeping bag
Cracked twigs on the path, fragile

Yesterday the mockingbird was deaf
Enter freedom
Telephone to the stars
RED on white and blue
                                        Bongos on the roof
                        Brando on the waterfront
Blisters from the dew
Idiot stew
Cohesiveness, a flash
            Of deja vue, a dream

                            Recent rodevue connected
                                        Hurdling towards
            The Holy Grail
                                    Winds howling
                                                secrets
                        of economy and pleasure
as Prosperity dwindles
With n ustice, pre judice and
  Greed that keeps the nation strong
lust inside me shallow
    Fruitless barren passing fad
  Howling mad to no end pleasure
      What buys pleasure?
orifice of reason?
  Who can transform
            these destructive
  Winds
  howling to themselves

Secrets rattling
 cracked windowpanes head splitting
 Below rafters creaking
pillars shaking
 There is no hiding
Come out to face
 the storm to
 Void the norm cozy withering Stand in the rain
                                    with me, I've got

        promises
                       jetting   grand burdens
            of all humanity to bare
                         reigning myself waning
           church bells clanging
           Vengeance in the name
            of justice Will the meek inherit
           the Earth?

woman in pain to give birth
I feel your scream
Father what will your child see?
Who will he be?
Will he grow
 gardens, kill weeds
                                    or drive a bulldozer?
Declare war? Love the bomb?
            Get mediacharged til his brain is numb

                            ?

46

Rain again is falling
On the inside I am dying
Pitter patter on the window
Idle chatter from the grave
Reigns a love that's nowhere near
Burns a year of expectation
Nights of drink soothe days frustration
But who beside a mother mourns?
Who waits with open arms at morn?
The storm inside is thunderous
Outside the room is stale
The motions of our sorrows
Fill the air with silent wailing
At the pub the blokes go wild, Unlike a child I question laughter
Cause deep inside the echo chamber
I hear raining in the rafters
As I curse and classify
the falling rain and howling wind
smell of garbage keep me
Home from ever straying far
Filling me with motion rage
Garbage keeps my breath hot spewing
ill and damp damp and ill
From falling sky and frigid wind
Congested weak and dizzy
dizzy and weak eakly
from pictures no one really sees
Unlike crowds
unquestioning
Incapable of
making waves
Failing to chose I shrink to convention
Drowning in booze for escape and affection
fearing a shadowless life
and then death
As though humanity were a stranger
To a stoned creep reeking morality home alone
After a show
that no one knows.

47

a feather can arouse
   striking   a brick
                 is much too thick

      Pensive moments such as these
      Release a longing howling beast
     Out of the tweed, unders from Sears
          Rocks from God
Clashing
  Crashing
Dirtballs in perma press
       Hipsters on crosses   Bashing
   Spiked heads confounding
       Paperclip noose
      Walk beside me Modern love
Don't fret pretty woman
     This is no nuclear death
Just everyday, our own little worlds
                  Celestial black hole
Will the feminists exploit me?
              Does my barber know the style?
  Will my feminist exploit thee?
          Does thee barber know my style?
Need a new place   Not enough space
              Don't have time
   Who's this lone celestial creature?
      Telephone ringing
    Hop messy drowned head
    Is it alright in our herd?

     Tentative encyclopedic vacuums
     Pulling me into the machinery
   Staring at Earth through cold quiet space
I believe I feel
       about to pass
             Into the beyond

48

**Game
Plan**

sane
man
get
sun
tanned
and
swim

49

Scrambled messages
Cancelled friendship
Toward the mountain looking over
I can almost smell the view
Rich luxurious benign
Triviality toned down
Reality heightened
Snare drum funk in an alley at
Two in the morning when the moon is full
Live
Just a little Love
The music of our day
Media consciousness
Computer disease
There's no fightin' technology out of control

50

Leaving the bar
Driving a car
Before night's candle melts
To meaningless morning
Counting the trials
Until the bar

Counting the miles
Until the smiles
Driving the car
Into a bush

A summer eve
One tranquil tease
Blooms on the shore
Of sacred lore
As thick as paper
As cool as
Skating rink toes
In Minnesota winter

Tighten your collar
Stick up your nose
My arrogance shows
Draining
The car battery
My only ride
Home.

51

Sounds like Mr. McGoo got the hiccups
Oh no!   Stoned to the bone   Where am I?

You don't find yourself out on the road y'know
I'm never going back to retail.

Out of water
On the highway
Rock'n roll turnit
Uploud

Independence on your heart
Fancy car cruising bars tooling
Puddling poodling difdak
Donald the mod rod
Julie Joe jammin
Bangin on the whim whams
Love smokin'
Freaks

Everyone got their
Gravy day lays it all for two minutes
Became a brilliant dose
Of reality
That soon dissolved back unto
Routine mediocrity
And the banner cried, torn
And the apples rotted in wild weeds
certainly organic
Was the cream of hallowed eve
A preparation to
Appeasement of
Larks marching unto freedom
Wanting to free the Earth
Whoops
To claim immortal fame to
Dine upon all humankind
Flesh consuming, life controlling.

52

Julio played with the Earth like a ball
Hooray! He cried Hooray! Let's pop balloons
(It's got a hallucinatory effect, such play)

Julio trips with the radio on, singing
I'm a remedy for the pain
Brains for folly, bouncing wonders, weightless fears
Julio stands in the rain with no umbrella
Lovely, isn't it? He cries, Jolly lovely

Julio gets a slap by a sinister
Minister speaking on suffering and death
Julio opens his eyes, feels his flesh crawl
        Running for shelter and out of the drain
Some noble hobo hits him up for some change
        Gives him a curse for his blessing
Julio falls in the bar in depression
        Julio waits in the dark for a light
Julio, Julio, who's lover/doctor?
Daybreak comes and he makes humble strides

Standing in the pain with no umbrella
Julio faces fate with resistance
Away! He cries with a shield of importance
It's got a powerful effect, such play.

53

The closer to death
The closer to life
Opposites become alike
In darkest moments
Shine brightest glimpses
Suffering meets comfort
Hate meets love
Future and the past
Divided by the present
Will soon become one
When living is done.

54

She likes to dance, I don't mind
Noticing her legs are kind
She's a bitch to what she doesn't know
But afterwards she's curious as
Extravagance wailing in misty moonlight
Aren't we alike?

I come to the pub to shed my disguise
And share my
Extravagance

Would you like to nibble on this dribble or
Ride off into the sunrise?

Truth and sorrow, soil and worms
We decompose to feed some more
Take down the myth of lore!
Come in tune creature of
Creation blooming alien angles on
Earth is life is Earth breeze blow

Monogram us

Dusty heat vineyard fresh
Rolled around the
Mortuary
Toolshed
Lounging
After toil and trifle
Improperly improvising microcliches
        Love
                Doves
a   Grass
blade   Trees
of   and The Hammer
marmalade
cost extra

Oh do I fear those empty towns
So bleak and unawakened
Undisturbed, such good people
                    Don't touch the cage or I'll scream
Scatter seeds
Everywhere
Grow your wild flowers   Burn baby smear
            Your sacred engines on the wall
Homemaker, Warmonger
Love, but I'm immune
Call me by my first name
Drop the last
My name is
Ms.

Now she'll be calling
While I'm out here crawling
Around in the jungle not
Sewing a roost

Getting at truth picking
Gazing at food wishing
Maybe the roof wasn't
Leaking at all

So high the famous tongue
Too much the jungle exiled
Once I laid on these shores and dreamed
Of leaving before
I left,

Now again I see colors
Belly growling, brain on fire
Sit back to rest and watch the
Highlights on
tv

I'll be moving forward soon
Sit tight tonight
Is immune

Fables and cradles
Crumb trails, art heaven
All leave me alien
All take their toll
On maidens and merrymen
Uneducated
To the gravy and recipe
Labeled as happiness

Price going up, let's drive in
Eat the G.N.P. before the F.T.C. calls the C.I.A. on us D.W.I.'s
We'll be D.O.A. During M.A.D. days.

55

Play with your toys til they rust

don't bother yourself much
Is why you get along so well
But trust me
The fog beyond the photograph
Comes from a hallway of art in question
And the hallway is empty
I'm stuck on that wall
Incapable of breeding
Everyone smiles as they pass
And pat me on the back
I have no limbs, flesh or sense
I'm a brick in a wall
I've no will, no balls, no choice
Have not I voice and mind behind?
Send no flowers to my gravesight yet
I've been at work but I've not lived
Oh I've had visions of living
Breasts to caress with no other thoughts blinding
Numbing my senses, preprogrammed -- A life

Can become so fucking compartmentalized

Void of comprehension and spice
Cohesion, sensation, appreciation
But oh can one lie smiling *"Everything's alright"*
Repeating trite words without giving thought
Why speak if not to enrich?
One ice cube dropped in a glass
Two ice cubes dropped in glass
Positioned under the kitchen sink and filled
with water -- Why
have a mind just to struggle? Why get by
 without reaping daylight?
Exploit all the moments, sniff dirt and sky
And don't take it with to the grave

Stuck on a cold old stone wall
Of humanity's ascent
If failed we lose it all.

56

Sun shines in East Berlin too
Love
Laughter, beer, good food
It's only a wall that hates

All soldiers have faces
And lovers tell lies
Those careful think twice
 of their battle cries
I've been on both sides
 and its only a wall
An ugly wall.

57

I cannot speak
Without fools' words
My summer spice
Has departed and I fear
Time fades all feeling

I wish to write
Though much too late
My apology for being
Unable to relate to what I sensed was
High above my disposition
As days became more than just passing time

Stubborn individuals are prone
To miss the warmth that others know
But who needs heaven when there's chance of hell
Why not just grin, pretending

Well,
All was fine til a finer come along
To ruffle up the feathers of a bird who'd forgot its wings
Jesus, what a bleak light life had been
And was again
Once a voice I couldn't ignore
Echoed through the walls no more.

58

Hey Big Bubbleloo,
Some demons got me I believe
Hey, don't be scared to read it -- just don't wanna burn my eyes
  my eyes my wondrous eyesore boat help sink drowned ooh
isolate can't ya fake it pretty well deceiving help oh help its al a lie
lie lie lie lie lie lie lie

Where is Earth?
        Am I really a creature?
I wanna cry with happiness before I die
I wanna do nothing else
And this is how I do it dammit
        passing the time
Writing cool lines bye dreamboat
In or out of it

Belly flop of sock hops sloppy sitting on a friend's wife's couch
Writing longer lines to use a lot more words don't isolate the
thought –

              searchin for a fantasy
              left after a few postcards
      caught a bus to Edinburgh and camped outside of town
              saw a great sun one long day
              on the way to Orkney
              got a ride from Sean Connery to the sea
              sensed some mystery and
              kept a distance from the local creed
              a giant wall devouring
              Eyes on coiled barbed wire fences
              On a battered bus to Belfast
              Dirty Dublin, Is the isle
              Really enchanted? How so invented?
              Machine guns myth Paris
              couldn't wait to begin
              Left immune to humanity
              The girls are all so lovely
              free

Amsterdam didn't get a chance

Not even with old friends
On the way to lonely Copenhagen
afraid to bare it all
out in the open through the thin ice
Fjords of reality
 meal the next day
I spent the night almost meeting a few
At the great train station.

59

Ready for this?
Peace with blisters isn't peace
This is the woods where we trip
Meat in the oven
Bleeding brains out
Blowing stout loose
Cutting nooses planning
Dreams spanning
Cities scenes eternities
Raining afternoons on Haight Street
Wide brimmed hats and army coats
To puddle through the mote
Yes,
It's raining now in old San Fran
If I was there, I'd be still in
 the void, black hole
 enviable, Out of control
Miserably Confused by it all
Trying to grasp
 at
Wisconsin.

60

Turn up the volume
We're playing hardball now
bewildered on a keyboard
Rubbing bloodshot eyes and waking on a warm double
 No heads to hear but old bearded lumberjacks who
haven't got so much new to say from day to day and in fact
repeat their facts within fifteen minutes

Ringing Hari Krishna cymbals

Sitting back to discover the scene
It got old within a week

Ug thugs wishing dudless blood conscriptionaires
Pears matched in perfect crates sardine wrapped
preceding your dreams
eyes closing, pupils dialating
destroyed
crashed

Is that all you've to say? Took enough words
What is it you're writing? Nobody knows
Thank god for the joint
I don't care, who needs God
Autotrophic swimming in the stew.

61

Departing now
Everybody ready?
It's Blast off time
Hang on tight
Vroom!
Whoosh!
Here we go
Streaks across the sky
    Colors, can we laugh?
    Cuddle on a mocking chair
Rocking nature
    Nomenclature
Blowing dust off wasted years
    Tear basking
    Flamboyant task
Winding clocks rocks falling
        Parading
On the toob boob nipple apple cherry
    Gotcha goo little gumrot tot bopper
            Fireworks for the emporer
        Crazed visionary's bridge
                Headbands halt exploding
        Expanding dandy
Lunarscapes discovered
Rattling through remainders
Of conversation sifted
Molded into makings of a brilliant Page apart

If life's the one art truly noble
What so solid is tonight
    in fear of ending
            Ringing engines wishful bones
        where hath the sky gone?

Cannibal clowns
Skyrocket bombs and
Little men get high, I
don't wish to agitate while
 man is on the make In the eye
of evil is A saint

                    why
            I don't even know
         If the writer wrote the show
       Or if thistles breed the flowers
      Will an earthquake fall the
         Towering
            Towering
       Giants with their hatchets
     Pioneers were wretched
        Like tomorrow, yesterday
     Cynicism sacred

Laid back
Sit around
Get high and trust the water
sewer pipes and faucets
What you eat is what you are
Fast cheap junk

Through the puddles
Trailing light
Further sight
The muse has made
me feverish
Delirious
paranoid, puzzled by
The size and hogging of the pie, I
seem to see that I will die
But who's to say and who
is Throwing rice at armchair figures
Dashing off to grow a heater
Trampling flowers every where cause

Bugs are in the air
beneath the polished floor
Fakin ecstacy askin for
So much more

I can see you're no bribe taker
And your mist isn't some light labor
Where you wanna go is the top
Of the bottom drawer

Glossy iced Colleen
Take your time pretty pet I'm not
Sexist I don't even exist
 anymore
Than The yellow pages or the bible
No tomorrow
 though
    maybe your baby
Can relieve an ancient life full
 of poverty impressions of
        Sacred misdemeanors
Steering clear of chaos

 now the night whistle blows and off
Are jukebox junkies
 collecting Lullabies to die
 and maybes to will to their
 heirs,   How many trumpets
                            do get high
              watching railroad engines blow
                    Out in the cold snow
                    Recording the range
                    Of microphone's strange
                    Power to change
            the way of
            hooray love?

Buggerman duke lude gage paging old
Homewrecking nincompoop wastoes on toast

mugger bread the night away go grocer grow
is thouest opening or no?

norm numbness nagging close
glossy gumdrop base flags
goose owl foul hoot moot point dull
shrill voice tune switch bored far
since tunnel confusion began poor tuck
 you in sin grease peace men shun nation bundle
honey O.A.M.C.I.B.U.D. invites you to
 booksales
burned barn sides loft lilly white hound dog
bound mad necessarily bad
noose with jam jail rusty frail scissorswail chop popping loghog
godtalk double meek sleek feat turn style

                    Sunday
        ?-,..."""-\ \ \so
        is this the mystery I've sewn
        all alone
        coyote high
        laser sky
        liquid sigh
        dust bunnies blow
        through ghost towns
        gold gone

            pillar fashion
            action ruthless
            hasty mix
            after remarking
            tea lamb trinkets
            bombs with crumpets
            leaf with bombs
            gray with noon
            boom balloon
        tampered saloon so dry butt rotting
          dotted along coastal properties
        devouring their theology   gray trumpet dented
                bass drum vibrating

                                        funeral profession
                        only in birth
Now
I recognize
 whispers Bloodshot and retired
away from film, til thin
the other fish are thrice
best with rice if   you wish
East guest   some guess   sprinkle taint
gash bus   brained gay
firm tush   away stay
pushed   cushion
              thatched pain

La-la-la   Deep murmur
 La-la   leaf warmer
  La   absorber bam thank you sam
   a mother gumbo   fart
        with a living room heart   started darting art
                        partway to the supermart
 gravy   navel   salvage   angry   basted
   love   knave   dangerous   faith
        anus   blame   gruesome
            lame   fashion
                    tart   start
       allegory constitution declaration abstract
            face place dating back to rare
              grocery rule pointer volume
      news   toe   lane   high   weigh   stable
          memory taylor fire save
        loose frank ball   rest
          cement fist reason
        insisting
                                    existing
                grace thou bliss
                    ter ace up town

made it late night empty dog
gone bag out fresh run thoughts was
friend call ballroom doom can custom
heart weep beeper flies out in through

leg won well fly cloud high style pig
figment cymbal dimple allowed dog hare
some three one your on Mars fun

                                   Never go
             away, don't question birth
                 I'm flogged by thirst
                 Sense lies down toe
             lap lucking drop by love bumps
          rally beast at last one three some
       that ought oontake complicated eaten
       blown over slow throwing ruins to croon
   sap stop rap happening not found

       christmas bizarre
       through yardburn brown eyes
       shapes of wrinkled brain envelopes
       soldier boulder sooty
       ground up in experimental air trip trap
       not a drop gained
       don't doubt swallowed chuckling
       all at the breakfast
       cherry converted
       leather

more numb limbs sleeping
   mountaintop teething
keep coming faith hopping
pen motion forward

pretty sour buckle sorry everything is all
right and wrong at the same time hold me
time that we might dream might told
takin kids away
 to wander
shoe lace dots at night hold
tighter studder torn

                 Here we go out party time
                 Skyblue grassgreen

Riptide
                    Torn away too quick
            Hold the mail stone clerk
            Glowing night can't bowl with bad rats

The freaks got fried
But keep on riding
 for kicks
The ocean's a lake

        Oh weren't we pretty
        Ice melts to mud
Umpteen sacrifices to mad dog society
        Revelation, revolution
How about me?

        Carpeting flying
        Disguised buttocks skies
Discontent buttocks talks
                    Apart from gleams of dawn
Green spiral bound pages rolling
                    Polling place spices
In fear of annihilation
Singing supremes
                    There's No MADness In The Twentieth Century
Love's as rational as balloons
Life always comes together too late
And only fate is exclusive

 a festive
 bright umbrella in the chaos shower
Trying to summit
 all up I wonder
If the weirdness is a blunder
Or the atom is the thunder
If it's all a myth
In the black
Bird's nest

The
Scarecrow
Beat it's chest
And caved in
One
Funky painted summer
By the sea

We
Forever strangers, dissolve
Into myth

                              Becoming
                   What wasn't there
As we sit and stare
Or glance around to grasp
 a glimpse Of harmless casual
 acquaintances again

Need our psyche's maintenance?
Western bore, whores and tophats
Coattails digging up the dirt, I
Am fearful for the Earth
Soiled water in the wake
Yet can I bare
To yield to fair, do I dare?

It's all parta my
Fife and birth, breath of cigarette
Pale of vice, let heaven be nice
we believe
In heaven and vice, hot air balloons
                    Immune
           Hinging on inklings
   Attacking castaway persona manifested
Atmosphere degenerating
                              If I can't make you smile
            Imbalance sinks harmonic

Unified

Existence?

Star Trek?

Chocolate cake?

Amazing grace?

Land tomb of the king
Doors closing silent

Or with a bang
Trying to be

Narrative
What good is nature?
One ends up being green
Compared to the movie screen

Dying, moving absent
Intake strange, is it change? Can I control
Being?
                                                    A retreat into the past
            I never found the magic bus
                        And nobody really looks at rainbows
                        It's just a dream they've got
                        Has something absurd
                        Called destiny to blur
                        And paint over our faces with scenes

                        Reality is anarchy
                        Teenagers are freaks, little darlings
            rulers of things catered to

                        Footsteps upstairs static attic
                        Raising the annie'll heighten the stakes
                        Freedom is alien, commune afar
            full moon a beaut but sober the crowd

Soon
The world moves
And stoops to listen
To the chords
Of yesterday's
Today

 to the heartbeat of America
Sponsored by
                        A game upon the shore
                        Is there nothing more?

                    Now I've spent my whole life searching
                        Now I'm spent and need retire

Hanging revolutionizing by the window on the street
Sweet sleepless hours with future to greet
    Good to eat girls all around, ego power
Star flower child Twinkling
            mind reflecting
 old loud proud and new

        Everything said may just be a lie

    Down and let the white bird flee
  His cage blowing in the frozen rain
   As leaves blow to make their connection
Communing with knowledge and opportunity Seeking
            an eternal apple tree
        Blossoming every spring
   Music that makes you wanna make music

        Fruit and inspiration
        In a golden cage, as some
        take the stage   To inspire
   another age
 Taken for a ride
On a demon tide
Inviable to the rose

Ask soft for why
art is the sky
Wheels turning clockwise
Disguising pivots

As bandwagon crusades
Grow forever on decay
If all that was to do
Was add spice to the stew
There would be no hungry
canons fighting
A fly patrols the ruins

Come in tune oh outward one

Or what's your vision?

Scent of confusion bloomin
Dire downpour soaring reign
Framed fantastique sheik leap
For applause and love

Does it matter mindless inconsistent
Should misfire lame tire score?

Bore no more Seas of dreamt harmonies
the Bees do as they please

In seasons of bliss, thought for a kiss

But a near miss weighs on the engine

Heart pumping cosmic crap ludicrous

Recited on television and scribbled

In bathroom stalls, tattooed on skin

Let me out or in

  the rain on the roadsign

  loud on my bile

long senseless miles

Bureaucracy talkin'

Red tape multiplying

  fine fascist dining

On blood and flesh wearing fur

Brrr! Did the lad begin

Hunted by a salmon's eye

On a giant crowded freeway sixteen lanes wide

A glass of gloom spilled on the floor

It started some time

Long ago.

sOuLfOoD tO gOgO

Bent out on another, eh?

S'this the summit or the pit?

Love turns you into superman
and then it hits

heavy bomb

wound and shatter

broken matters

again

Alien Confusion

don't know where dreams are going
don't know
what's come and gone

    someone shot the sky down
tearing the horn off the unicorn

        we go dancing,
            the back alleys of Venice
    Lurch in his golf sweater while the crazy woman
            lost in her world of salvador dali
    spins allusions

    as we dance laughing
    passed the wicked witches candy house
        letting towtrucks pass
don't know
if the walls have soul
               or these people
  feel as they fill the crevices, don't know
if metaphysical dilemmas form the core of life or
 if i'd be better off in san francisco,
                  I just don't know
plainly
what the hell's going
on

Blooming confusion chaotic and alien mass vibrating uncertainty
shriveling and dying curled up on an unmade mattress
in early eve as downstairs they play
trivial pursuit and have
a blast
   i don't know
 if this all can continue anymore
it takes its toll
 no mortal island, not easy to conform
to fast food marauders, maniac consumers
play acting as if it's real

I'll create a world filled with
warm hearts encased in smooth flesh wanting to act
out private fantasies, directing
desires to the problems of humanity as i reflect
on what it is i'm missing by not being
somewhere else.

taking it all out
with the garbage, pass the butter
to
the deserving few

where are they to be found?

coming right out of the woodwork
diving in discrete ideals

titillated by

fate.

desert mirage

city of smug smoggy traffic licking smiling beautiful people

pictures of beach perfect near bodies conforming not hidden

los angeles city come quickly!

sickly

los angeles

non grata

los

angeles

los

angels

lost

                    spread apart and packed together
             weak end days racing by on the free ways
                breathing toxic chemicals speeding
                              to
destinations unweighed: It's no wonder
everyone
                    races fro and to on endless
                              freeways disconnected

this is nowhere

and there's no place to go

             sun shine's bright
                    but still I can't find
no

soul

                              and there's no place to go

                                             cut off
from good soil and such all
                    dressed up inside too many walls entertained
by recorded music
                                             images
                        plots
                              messages

cracking like decoy ducks

hoping on luck
Siphoning it all up

loving

ingrediants expediant

as afterwards

intertwines

lullabies for deserving eyes

                                hit or miss sacred

alabaster ate it
choking up cough puke
pollution to groove on
corrosion/amputate
       put 'em up magistrate!

i've no solution've you?

enjoying stew
                                   sewing moons

 glowing gloom booming
                        up suburb meat
    clean as sheet
white sale
       tagged special!

kissy on cheek, oh
it's cozy
honey.

       (funny
      average folk got it all
screwed up like the rest)

                                          .

The Beer Man Calleth

The beer man calleth
 and go do I
  towards another drunken dawn
  towards another another

There's a bottle in the fridgerator
 How I curse it, how it calls

I blame
Noble and sane
Society for being so fucked up to lead me to this
 dead end road;
How awkward it seems
 truth gets scoffed as lies unfold rewarded

so
 another curse extended from my cursed mirror.
 and all the ignorant do goody's get trampled on the path

The beer man calleth
 and I drowned.

hollyollylollyollywood

dreamland
loud modern would
should the right come along

follow the furor don't question
happiness

drinking divine
character alive
talkin chimney soot sweet apple pie
toting the line
snort easy dimes
ollyollyollywoodhol
tripping on the borders
suspicious of
the
viciously merry

light colors
seaside sun

once before the fumigation
there was what was isn't

new sycophants known from the smog created

sorry blisters
                  whispering
                              blues

        in search of wisdom and world news

to apply to the heart
shake that guitar

hour approaches trench replies
filled with cunning alibis

evacuated amusements dated
fading into jading unto

        known sycophants sorry from the smog created

each day
                            bound skies

      above a shiny new babylon drunk

once you've got a taste
ugly afternoon grooves out of place knowing

burp relaxed cause it's all on the way.

Wouldn't it be nasty if it all went down tube just right now?

Bye- bye braincells, chemtrain

talk mace for the bleary eyed

soul chaser makin coolie, tokin rovin mary wanna bake a tepee?
sale at the big one hold musturd trust me take to the beat stall the
heat take a rap to the bank shake hands with the big boys roll em
that what your were bred to do, and defend.

It was it was it *yes!* I can take a tulip to the brain gig
fizzle trickling like candy storms out of the sky, licking chop
children standing in line for the carnival rides.

Flashed before my eyes may you can we stay still?
      when how to
late bank on
     pig hank man be stool fool, ah shit
something
     is

    killing   me, tell ya what is is if

youll kindly communicate,

      with me

    (heart to heart, head to toe, soul to soul, honestly

I'll be waiting at the door in the rain.

)

radiation supreme

pray it ain't bleak pray
for the weeping to cease, but where? I hear not
weeping,

It's a sweaty night, I've been to the sea
 the fresh, cool wind is strong and now its dark

                                           but inland
god how i'm sweaty like a nervous lovestruck hick
which I am and
always will be if
I get another whiff
of
you.

who was irwin?

the silly man who's hair stuck out

that nimrod on a space cloud
dollying up to a tram

dot to dotting in perfectly formed colors behaving
like nobody ever could
like nobody ever would
like
     man,
          when it gets into to your head you wanna get a tan
man
          the language is so grand
   pillars of Columbia University
            in blue jeans bought off the man

cool handed
lost in the jive
         slapping all the way out, smiling

in mod space pods prodding old rerun plots

dated duds hustling old

yesterdays

' diddly squat flute muted moans.

What's so sacred about saturday night?

                    h
    y
        t

    b]

                         q   s
                         d g f u j k l p i v c k w

    f y u i mp d s w e

    what's it all for?

            what's itall for?

                what's itall four?
                    whatzitalfr?
                    watzitfr?
                wtztfr
                            ?

dying for a thin page
drawn up on a strange screen, deeply inbedded

damning the tackiness needed to make contact
communication to a mirror

magnified

by day by night
two separate lives
in one the dreams relieve
in the other they're believed

no more romantic dreams no
more

tied neck consumers everywhere
media clones unaware

what strange poverty is this?

CAPITAL MOLD

fuckin money
stalemate without it

so what do we learn?

Earn.

sofotogogo

we're in the mula
soul food go go
we're in the high life
in
the big top.

dressing up we're
going to town
in a clean car
steppingh i g H.

These shadows fucking move!

Get the axe

                                        and the hammar
            Blown up in a swell fiasco
                        two good timing shoes never trusted
                sincerity was a trick, wasn't it?

                        Heart beating bloated
                        Too much trite cocaine
                Whiskey and rambunxion
                        Whatever became

                        Of noble
                peace dreams dated?

            They say its in the past now, cut your hair and suntan
                                            go to vegas
vacation dude

                        load a CD in the auto
                            get some gas
                        and take a trip
                            quick

passed fast food
at eighty miles an hour dude
across the SoCal fun-shine cruising

watching postcards pass.

This isn't where it began
this is suntan
this is damned
This isn't romance
this is but a bargain to dance
with
you who the piper longs to play for
you who warm the stew
toiling for truth
and
ah
e
atom cloud icon clad as sadistic cross thinking gross protruding
nose
classical
plausable
fantastically enlightening
as
racing blind lovers catch grace
moon soon marauders wear lace
to the hollow show
finding no shore
to latch onto and rearrange
beguiled mares of night
mistaken for voodoo, bewildered by charm

and so it goes
and so it comes to pass
as so it seems
and soon it doesn't matter again

as though it weren't
and then it is all over again
somebody put it all down
thus making it wise to conform to.

streets empty

trees perfect

ly straight and shaped

squares

and spheres

even

cut grass

talk pleasant

please don't make any noise,

stay   the night   but fake

delight

when buffoons steal the

heart

the   loon   soon   shoots   the   moon.

nobody ever did one a favor
by letting it all steep towards the graveyard

its part of the gravy to slave for and maybe
someday soon apple pie 'll be delivered
by a lover arriving at the backdoor at noon

but don't count for a savior
when it gets out in the open
it'll all be public scandal

nobody ever did one a favor
polishing gold hearts
  to snipe at the unclean : - -   -   -

after dinner
take the movie for a thrill

take this pill to get you

                        o f   **f**   **f**

escape

        to fantasy.

graceland

shrine to the king

guarded, not given away

from out in the backroom island darlin lost her
garland

o.d.'d on fame

how close is fate
to the cradle?

graphics that cannot compete with tV

I can't help but be true
to my inner mood

ego unit grips like a handgun
so much fun it shouldn't be
powered by a fearless timepiece
racing off to distances unweighed
by harrowing minds

zap zip zip zap

hustle out to tempt the mote man
he says the neighbors all got one
jungle's full of tugboat ding dongs
hung under movie marquees

Puppeteer above the rafters
no one knows who wrote the show
leave the fame to beauty suntanned
that's the way it doesn't grow.

AhhhhAHhhhhAhjHHHH!

keeping
portraits of bygone eras
dusted and sunproof

death preserved

life remixed!

its part of the gravy to slave for baby

tuned to sitting mock n stroll vibrations sheltered from
                                        smog engrossed fun
Basking in the quarry sun full of demands
Bowie's got a teardrop painted in his eye

I can't see the sunset cause I'm way too
                              H i   g h
        and the mountain don't get grander
                          Dawns are a fucking drag

              spiritually starving while

here inside the machine tuned
To video and audio and
pausing limelight

strapped down beneath the moon

as the bullet train races

coming at

y

  o

u

consumer bloat

flirtin with the abstract hoping for redemption
flogged by inambition-sniffing patrols repressing freedom

safe inside the mote toting middle aged flubber like a damsel in
disguise
scratched from the howling in the street last night

from the id shouting spouting out to peaceful neighborhoods
youdrunksyoudrunksyougoddamndrunks go strait to hell and let
us get some sleep would ya please dammit god damn

ookay but gee

its nice to see the whites of your eyes in the moonlight.

take me

from pits of indecision past the movie screen
in tune with all things living to hear
                                        music of the sphere
drop the codes that cloak the flesh!
trying to be top dog
trying to be the boss
                                        take me
                        away through the out into, away
                        forever
            the monster to escape is me
                        how far must i travel to be free?

i am all living things
connected and released through me
my bond to the cosmos eternal
                                at dinner waiting for the check
                        at a nite club sneaking in the back
                                            take me
to the heaven of my dreamy stride   let me
hear the birds with true desire and completeness
disrupt the corrupt programmed video sense deprivator
                        for oh how i long so to soar on the wind
while fearing not my destiny unsacred,

Saturday, a new frontier, another beer for breakfast
Wasted place doth show on face in cracked mirror

the year becomes trampled in a race
and will this pace and research turn the heart into a pacemaker?

and will a shiny automobile please and inspire the neighbors?

how could my garage be bigger?
How can I buy the women on the pier --
                awaiting material princes in yachts?
never mind love

could i take another trip? is it time
is that's what's secretly been on my mind?

bullshit!

here is where i am where
i'll stay

                                        awake

                here
                      i can't escape
simply

                                    rock'n roll

familiar

                                    destined stroll

                      trying to break the mold

we can feed the sea
of indecision
or be

we

can dream

disease

hang outlaws
inlaws

hang around in the spectator corral
going around and round

                                  inside walls
                    painted with murals called freedom.

zzoom

swooosh

dasshhhhh

bz

scscscscscscssssssss

hazel

dead bolt

brass handle

gun
un
nap
at
two
woo
choo
moo
n

job
fair
wheel
big
slick

s
ad

i can dream i can
scheme forever making plans for fara
way a

head

lettuce

chakras

devoid

guru

drinking and sinkin' into yellow lead pencil

delinquently dreaming
of affectionate tomorrows,
There's a man here smokin' on a big cigar
Calling on the telephone
Ringing on the collar

There's a man here
Rambling on about injustice
a man, or so he thinks
somehow beyond us all, besieged in his mind

by abstractions that come too be known as life
Manufactured into
reality
Confused by all this talk of survival
For who?

Few
glimpses

of cohesive peace
so vital.

dangling on a farm fence

grandpa's got a prophesy
        ain't that just the way to be
seeing wisdom through the lines
taken back to Custer's time
slaughtering in the name of God
silent at the bar

zoned out by a television
drinking with my silent friend
as i regret drinking
and i regret being here
as i regret ever being heavy
and i regret not being with you now
i never read camus' the rebel
and i never
walked
the yellow brick road
never assumed there was a path to heaven
not, at least, since that year of transition when
i learned
that
nobody lives forever and
women are painfully more
than angels

now seek me like all the geeks
flesh and substance to sustain the
cue-
yews

whiskey for the maddog trying
to break the machine of its kinks

I hear motors hissing
mechanical brains beeping
as i wonder why should i
get out of bed in the morning   ?

stroke the babe toke late and keep calm embalming
on toast bringing bread and butter fed on utter
ances nice vice bad jam
last scam a known'son romance grown
dim
wit
hath flown
as
a
favor to the throne

tempted to
bank anew
with a few more thieving magpies
taken for too many rides
stop the game!
it's a shame
all propelled and swelling
deceived and smarting
bargaining
for
revenge
ohh, I shudder
truth
is hard
full of clutter
angry afternoon
take me from this room on a magic carpet ride to the moon
dark and lonely lowly warm me take me
out of the underground into the light

                    stage fright
                    has worn thin

generosity akin
to skin radiated
basted in steroids to perform for
Toxic Norm, Plastic Surgeon

birds aflight in vanquished skies

peace was alive in former lies

stains in the empty cup left on the floor

Hail to the chief!
But who the hell is he?

Squeezing through crevices of the mold
Soulfood to go go go
Aloof inside the cockpit searching for the promised land
Grab hold of the tow rope
Whiskey is for the kid
making constraints
on what might have been missing
no one can take twisted hissing away
or can they?

adulthood incomplete
staring gogol-eyed at writings on the wall
wanting to tear it
down
caring
only for wares
barely catching vacant stares
nightmaring with a few
who
dip into the strange wild brew
defeating cares in winterland
recreating
procrastination
sunken from
a weighted pat
on the back from yesterday
as it passes

away
today's mocking
took its toll on painters pallets

fucking hell
funkin cool
groovin' stool
national stall
banking hours
petty toll
toking   on   the   moon

          santa   saint   father   fame

attic   indigestion   antagonistic   heaven

          say it ain't   so mo   say   it ain't

G E N T R I F I C A T I O N

                                        take a time trip
               getta mind fix
                         willing to destroy
                              all the profound joy
                                        and life will be
a comedy again
foolish like the rain

mysterious, unvain
grooving ignorantly forward
                                   let the consequences sink
               the weight paving the way
          as whimsiness ignites

                                        profoundly
     make it be
                    rich don't

               let your culture twist my aims

love leads the only light of day

i want to sing you love songs
in the bathtub
and dry to write you a novel of love

awakening

fearful

waiting to burst
to leap

                                    to be alive

take me on a drama
forget the numb norm nagging close
running through the sky
to mimic hidden cries inside the soul

of light, oh no
come out oh spirit touch

but the brilliance fades
grows a cold wall
painted great.

straight to the heart
shake that guitar

love's an illusion
god is love
i made god.

      Such pleasure dwindles
burns
  solidifying vacant stares

                                 encouraging a loss
ah,
but no one wants to be a fool laying their heart on a barbecue spit

nobody takes a shake
passed
the elephant idol, a misguided matchbook
the un-escalator? portable vibrator
insect repellent, we're not
crazy after all
lazy, but it's true
I'm so in love with you
decadent whore bitch slut get outta my hair
care bear bunch brady gonna take-a-maybe-days-loveboat
vacation

fucking hell

now that my head explodes, expands

got the lingo and the suntan

when will the internal blisters heal?
or the good fairy grant

or the deserved crown?

heartache across the telephone wire
dust in the attic

baking dry in societal molds
chasing gold
en dreams
legend high movie screens.

OBLIVION OPUSCULUM

Take away my past, the present's gone

Ah, marvelous shit, but endearing, yes

You lost lost lost lost lost lost lst tsl o s t l o

That's the way we go heedbobby ridin down on custard saw the
lighted alimo drinking like a stig pink in a stye rink where the
y'knows hang out questioning gravy and alamo and lord custard's
got too much mustard on his mashed potatoe pumpkin pie.

When we was we, we used to be free as could be.

Now its just a riddle why bounce your brain around with
tennis rackets.

Soon they'll come for more more, well fuck it I ain't
gonna take it no more
no fuck society, I retreating to the woods.

Sorry about my misconduct, my fucked up sincerity my,
grumpiness towards abstraction my, lost redemption search
that never will produce
or will we can we be friends after jet airliners scatter us across
the sea, up to the death star, over Mars, deep inside
                    the sea?
You may find, like many
That too much sugar is
really sweet

Or The root of the symbolic sentence was just a lazy way out from
recruitment into the societal zoo
                                        Well,
I surely don't wanna see
call this the blind poem, the wham nbam, the naked lunch that
Tarzan beat his chest for
jane on the vine
chimp made three,

butter up pancakes, please pass please
old toast with sentiment butter
got a bake sale on the way
please pass please pass don't
pass
out

just
be pass
ive and every
thing will be all right
they swear
by god says it'll be all right
to god pray and I heard them say they read a bout it in the news
today.

So, there weren't much point
in searching after
all

if I've found heaven, hell it stinks

Angry son of a homewrecking blew it up this time time time
sailed the big rhyme out of the regime
and now as I flirt with the silence of madness,
I bow passed reflection in hopes of redemption
                                    I lay my soul to you down angel
          Nowhere
Are to be heard the slow roar and hiss of the sea
 some poetry
          the prairie breeze
    city shooting out of the fields
                          minneapolis, when

will freedom once again raise it's head open it's ears, pop its
eyelids wide and stop fucking dreamin?

          and why the wide, bewildering spice of rye and wit?
          seeking accomplishment beneath the aggravating race
shouldering up to the smoldering thinking
this cannot be the end

                    and it seems so easy, here we go
                    over the edge and down in the pit
            feeling flesh rip across the coarse earth

what was an on looking widow to do but wonder who he
was and if this has been repeating over and over, brought on by
the devil himself. Hey, good hash, cover yourself with the trash
canned on your way don't step over the garden, on your way
through the beautiful, gee life is strange, the pianist pauses then
freaks bewildered on his keyboard,

                    Oh it was doomed to wreck you that's why
            society is to Limit creative potentials,
                    sucking up to ripe capital farts that come
from the bus, keep
that's what everybody's out to due
the in trim
is a
tin drum

tapping
tapping

as on a wood stage sleeps a man on a chair
where a waiter takes his last drink away

subdued gives way to silence
where do we go from here?

it's all been a frontier
but now the borders are down
and life isn't hanging on a museum wall

eclectic the many and few
coming to roost without
a
tool
machines turning rusty screws
for adieu

the dampness glooms.

and so the story goes
away

       attracted by
        the outward lies

 inner dues
upon the muse
  fusing

at last the age is but to say

a
few

to save
for

you

clues to
digging
the honest blues.

vehicles are comfortable deceit

i cxheat bu tonly to conform
to all there is to conform to:
madness
holiness
vagueness

emptiness complete

for now and ever
no past no future

                                no deceit

smile
you're on candid
camra.

No More Dying

Searching for a thoroughbred
camping on a rosebud sled
chatting with a cardboard box
getting onto knocks and kicks
then there is
when the big
commercial symphony begins in traffic,

junk in the trunk
skunk in a magazine
funk in a convent
new day's a comin', oh Soul Mama
are you ready?
take me home
I need
no more alien stew, lend me your
hand, lay your death arms down
are you ready?   to blow your bubblegum
in the wreckage
are the tempted
ready
for a workday
seems the foreplay didn't work
last try might be a little shy
are you ready?
to take the street, can you
bag it all up for the nice lady?

is it sit down time? Sitcom crime
dwindle fig moan,
farm on time frost
wheel borrow a cup
big steal amuck
on sale

no prisoners
incomplete

no surrender no retreat

fer all the funked out junkies
I'll claim the beach

trashed beercans afloat in seas of drifting moods

for all you maniac consumers
i'll sink gumdop heaven in a jar just out of reach

for all the
  game groovers i'll dig a deeper mote

gravy filled with a question of flavor for

                    all the souped hip hotrods homewrecking

i'm mute,

This cowboy ain't attracted to the loot
no necktie to reform beneath fluorescent office light

 famous last words
for all the material girls

flashing on scenes closer than big dreams
fighting billboard skies

while hoping apple pie.

dallas
got the new wave kites

tangled in a powerline

memphis
checkin the speedometer again

lately
seems the long drum beat
tilted
and spilled bones of the mellow buffalo.

wrapped in animal fur and a warm beer blubber
soul folk hat with a pheasant feather

dining down at the mission kitchen
with a good time gang ain't worried
that it's long been
Necessarily conditioned
to replace the air.

Blandness is everywhere
up the stairs
in the elevator
on the loudspeaker
up your ass
everywhere
be a Pig
let it stink
be alive
let it grow
groove on truth
be uncooth
if you wish
or get a clue
as to
what
is going
on
and
on so
can you take a joke?

a world beyond your swimming pool

odd art coves, shelters from
Noah's ark

                                   So Mr. Honesty strikes again
 spiders on the machinery
truths that pierce the heart and blow the mind
         hey,
                   that's the way it
     goes

boned

atlast we got them buggers
tuned
to fast food consuming marauders pruned

weened on digging dated crazes
face to the floor up wall warm gravy

alibi don't say it with your eyes
keep the disquise tight try hard with all your might, best foot
forward

                     sorry,
        I can't help but be true

                         to my inner brood

           Take the castle off the crown and who's the clown?
Bake pasta and we'll see who is the fig
  who digs a monday morning
  who longs to live?
   who just may be still longing
     to

    give?

tell me mister minstrel what it is

      at a bake sale, some old goody grandma poisoned kids
with too much sugar
                    while men in suits
        buzzed on caffeine
    came after the potheads
                     making them piss in jars
  crying
        "Religion is salvation not opium.
            The world is black and white.
              And I know what's right."

Slavation is not my opium!

Society's npt nearly even blue and black

and I know I'm trite.

                            as the fake gets
eplaced by the real, Oh what is?
   q.
   z.
   x.
      == \ ++ |
      @ff % & jojo
trying to get a head
hadagotta go back without a chance
withoutta clue$@#$%#$%^$#%&#$^%&&^% |+_))_+&^*(
so hard it can be
crucify me

                Turnit Uploud
learning
mousetrap harbours
                                              just an intercepter
                  trying to reach the highest ground
tee-pee down
bloodstained past
bleak mirage
desert present

labeled as gravy
icing on the make

cut those golden locks
get a job
groove to the hit parade

knock upon the golden gate
rock with the mountain
then
when
it's cool to lose
claim the blues

setback

soultester

character builder

crybabykiller

setback

soldier awakener

This was the heart

of the sun

spoken

for fun

amidst

triviality toned

pretty insecure in love
partially obscured by doubt

thanking the cashier for the deal
taking it all in, driving away

no baby food cake for desert This Time it's

fresh scent of oxime
gleaming white teeth

eating the right foods
doing the dishes on time

those were the days

sometimes i get so sick of
driving and such that i waddle to
and fro
combing
my hair

drink rock'n roll sniff peanuts
eat age up   yum yap

turnit uploud slash the cash for the bash grab some tush
       cram tugging slugs bugging
       touching around all night all right jump chance
       home

       no no No NO!
       wanna tune in now to the world
       inner muse too heavy

       wanna touch

       don't feel the room growing on budweiser bullion
       taste great no flavor
       i want a crutch

       wanna tune in now to the world
       wanna

       hang on to feathers as they fly

       boomdoom ExplodE

               W O R L D W A R I I i

       love is like an atom bomb.

staring
        at the vacantness just staring
    off
    at

fine

      fine!
such a fine you are i say
i divine
you are fine

you divine
i are
      fine,

blah ah ah ah ha ha ha!

bursting at the seams
clean rocket to

beyond the stars

more white space than a minute

willit

willit come together willit?
willit fix the blender willit?
stall the vendor tax collecting willit?
ease the blisters willit?

willit wondering top dog to relieve the top dog stains paging
  over clover heads bewildered angry thinkin failure

willit say come quickly and be painless sure as fire drowned
knock-down sincerity egged on out of wack swift dawn aging
on friend toast out of bread stale crackers

willit say stay the night tight shudders melting in elite screams
played out for ominance defending ignorant cellmates
        saliving on wedding cake

okay this caste shop talking bored with detail ram rodding more
ever much too more can't stop coping hoping for more
more more
what a drag the aggravate

more more more longing loving lurking irking quirking sand
quack dated fads heaven faded lately ate it stayed up too late for
nice dreams in sound sleep snoring yes I've discovered tv and
dinners two car garage paper neck-tie leisure suit barber
conformity for the wow girls gone flirting danger here she came
its my own fault I gave her the buzz
Now what waits

Willit bee
sedate nostalgic looking backwards ever no out of place snorting
haste cruising swift ventura freeway talking giggles burning
puzzles lettuce real world fade into a dream neglected for style
class amusing foreign sportscar substance demeaning to the soul

sorry samantha spin my gears in lovely none knowing but seven
years ago rowing on through thwarted weirdoes weren't we
expelled from heaven knowing what its made of surely we
can humpty dumpty put it all together again

i dream of seven eleven francisco san city brain bud rooftop rain
fog restroom passion whiskey danger motormadnecyle dew green
grass golden gate haight architecture old charming romance by
cliff north beach house mission postcards tackling old niners
party skipping to newness

willit take the car fine its a beaut runs good body great good tires
and miles miles i been so bored these past few months where ever
does that damn fucking good time glow go?
willit remain so?
willit go go?
willit grave the sea to dance for free in relief of video and greed
computer oozing yeck and slime changing flesh and awning lime?

honking horn hunk morning worn
won warm gone for now game over ever same old song story
blues glory brain must be stained for good
-bye goody yuppie yippie hippie hip take apple jacks and kiss the
toads goodbye
                                                                take me

willit be like tomorrow yesterday balancing on this and that
 rafter high abstraction shit cherished to perfection
alienated staying indoors living close to the beach where little
disquises tits and totties crotch and long limb muscle
hairstyle eyes hid behind sun glasses and ears always cursing
buried in amplified distortion

willit be quick and painless do i wanna get another suicide note
over with and hurry on to heaven now that my brain is anchored
once again by ever silly self important destiny designed to project
appealing to all hermanity

willit be just another quick trip big deal lye about the good times
no adventure returning home to nine to five dissolving into
photos forevermore?

is this the mystery i've sewn all alone consumer high guilty sigh
redemption flying out of reach on the beach preaching back
to those who see it not as i for who the fuck am i supreme to?
Willit?

willit damn willit cure purify add to reduced delusion guilty can
truth be magnified?

ah shit old inescapable alibis dammit shit fuck hurl the hurdles
 over the pale ale don't skin your knee on the track
spectator shitting on the bench
masquerador in a trench, its raining

and the music muscle turns to mud
a funnel cloud comes into view
the masses flee in panic just like pearl harbor
amusement park sirens ducking in the trench beside the roller
coaster scoping wet t-shirts eating picnic baskets ranger sir
heart attack grease blows it all away praying
to willit to willit woah, willit woo willit stall as it all hits
the fans blowing wreckage around the yard twister not one
not two but three holy rollers just the size of oz wizardos
vehicle syphoning the dust covered culverts as kids scream from
trenches flee from ma and pa seared scared praying
praying hard and mighty dignified noble hobo hoping to believe
and suddenly the storm is gone and all is eirrie
silent birds begin to meakly sling the sky still covered mud
eirrie and the children thank god

willit always be this way willit be banned forevermore to cruise
the launching pad as dated?

willit wonder ever be enough to replace dreams?

will the human brain succeed will blossums always bleed willit
always be willit in the end who sees the doomslayer poking
 thorns out of rose pedals willit be ever the end?

eVoLuTiOn

yEAH HEY, WHOAH YEAH DADDY WHOAH HORSE

sO WE GOT ENEMIES, fOES AND BIG TOES THAT STICK OUT

yEAH WELL GET YOUR SPIRITS RENEWED INSIDE

lET IT ALL HANG OUT

fOrTUNATE MAMAS CAUGHT IN SUCH DILEMMAS
tAKE THEIR PROBLEMS TO THE BANK

aND wE
sO MEEK AND DEPOSED
gOT NO SUCH LUXURY BuT CAN TRANSPOESE
fAIRY TALe FEAR IN THOSE WHO
lOOK TOWARDS THE SUMMIT TO PROVE
dESTINY

Duty Roster

gushing

through gutter greed puddles pure splashing pilgrims
trying to get on with our created worlds
spilled
all over the baby bib crib for hell's hecklers to tease

please don't think it's the faults of good folks
as long as you mean well all is clean
as long as
the
out
house is
scrubbed

spotless
SO
RIGHT
ON
COMFORTABLE
IN SONG
DEFORMED SPORTING
LOVE
A LONGING NEVER REALIZED
A STRONG PARADE OF ALIBIS

and this is what we win
truth
unabstracted, lonely
from seeds we hope will grow
bulldozed by

(I hate to say it but its true)

conformity

Leave no trace
 of subtlety be bold
think of lost ways
fathomed, labeled and let go
                in favor of
                        the way of

(I hate to say it but its true)

awakening today.

h.b.
soon to be a sequel
return beneath the planet of the misbeggotten part II

in 3D
one step closer to the real thing
soon we'll give it all up
permanently distracted

                                                op nyr pos os

dizzyzzd zzyid diz dzzyi

contrivance two
bluer than true
for slickers to bait the pilgrim haters
master bribe takers
calling the new dumb waiter a bore
for all the template whorer stories told
after midnight in white and black tuxedos else
maybe baby'll sees it all in context

                    ooh la la
                    strange how the cow bought
            his new car on dope

        lately the air just
        isn't remote

                soon the new woo will not
                wonder

        or wander

                                    piddling
                                        puddling
                        daddling in
.ifdaymiansumeroffspring
        so
        blow the man down dirty stoke up the town lordy hold on hold
        out hang the phone up call your mama baby cry and smear daisy
lown chains with
        the wind taking yourself for a ride on a golden tide true as blue
        summer nights basking in day working play for no feast trade
        tamed for a soul mate or
        sometime next weak
        make a

        peep

        asdllskhfjow3ientfjvnzjnq[er-90324582=39568ujrmvq83r cd

        Look at my foot
        at your foot look
        see veins? see blisters?
        see what you wanna see
        see what you cannot see
        oUTLINED
        Against a background world

DELICATE DELIVERY
anxious ambiguity
bold sensitivity
solid in harmony discrete
conjured up

by little feats.

*

saturday, a new frontier, ANOTHER year
damn disgusting looking for
the same old thing

head off pillow
beyond the jive
love playing with fire

what is real?

It's suicide, is what it is
i want to live

and suicide's only a metaphor for
suicide, nothing's real

                              anymore

touch the weight bench and the iron rail
          on the spiral staircase socks
and shirts scattered on carpeted next door neighbors

                how can you say that
        nothing is real?

ray gun   Z a p p p

        grip it

                rasp failing

                        into black hole of nothing

saturday, a new frontier, another year

once again dawned to juggle rickshaw bullshit

    trying

to groove with elements as cynical vibrations turn
to humungous bewilderment
            gonna get along in this eat doggie dog contraption
                        gonna
                        smooth out the wrinkles and let time

expand

B usted up

Downtrodden

Hot Sun

Blazing

I can't take it no more now not
                          afraid   of   nothing
            merrily merrily

by the oceanmightyocean roaring scoring

   storing up for owing

lazybones

mediocre

comfortable

wherever

what would you say?
about the trite titled children
if they showed you the way
to
heaven?

you know it ain't breezin'
in bed for a bleak peace filled art piece

i think you should bleed
its a rainy day soul

for all the going down strolling

coffee?
be guest
breast feed the nest

a woman is way too complex
to be labeled as trite
political economic religious sex occupational fruit
traits are just fragments

compartmentalized
conformed to
                                    breathing air and growing
                                        multiply knowing

            this brain's no smart computer
            i'm no mere rush hour commuter

    to that artist commune by the sea that i've been dreaming of,

hand picked

                        grown free

        believe?

an asset answers back
all is antsy after facts backing

big bang cross bingo

walk on hints

never close the door on friends.

poetry is

perhaps a noble

occupation

though the result corrupt,

the aim is pure

the aim will echo

fondling and caressing

erasing the veneer

tootie lutta

two tea lotta
marin yachta cali
for nigh eh
coat tin fall for
buskin strod lay
cool grim myat in
pool shearn haze
comfin full yearn
fide in learn tool
all of a yarn cloth
come ordained
oh la la la
oh la la
soon oh hustle brow
stern glow maybe knows
ruby and late fakin a lake
artifice altogether
glory glued to boring shucksters
huckfin gloomin bog buried
catchin a drift slow tide to lift
down wind pickin' up salamander
age changing hypnotists
rage chasin' gumball trysts
toast to cymbals & synthesized hats
eyes closed to moo cows
grazin' in grass green
cruisin' on swift screens
tears in teams of eyes anticipating
late dinner, ate along the way
train commuter poking up root
reading far off world aggravation
heard all before
toot eeh lotta
tittled loot
muscle groovstrong
now move the heart
all is art
doin dah-do, dah- dew dah
dum de-dum de-dum dum

Nature is Not For Cardboard Boxes

Winter Dreams

I dream of chopping firewood
Beside a log cabin covered in snow
Where out of the roof's stone chimney rises
Bellowing, sweet scented smoke

I dream of the fire warm inside
Where far from the city I reside
Sipping tea, hot brandy and cider
Snuggled close near the heat of the fire

I dream of the morning that follows the night
When I venture out to the winter morn's light
Through deep snow as piercing winds blow
To frost red my cheek, life then feels complete

Then I awake to city sounds
A drizzling sky and rushing frowns
When I awake I do it slow
I miss the Northern winds that blow
Miss the frost upon my cheek
I miss the snow that's four feet deep

I'd much prefer to fade back to sleep
To dream enchanting winter dreams
But today beckons to be redeemed

If all around was mad
I'd still have the snow
But there's more I have to give
Than my love for winter's glow.

A Heaven Before Someday

Early in the city
On a day called Sunday
Awoke by foreign voices
I arose to find
another life
Lurking
Outside my endless inner shell
inside another
partitioned box
With a view of
A neighborhood
To the sounds of
a neighborhood
Beyond my loved recorded music
beyond
The omnipotence in my mirror
My treasured fear
On a day
called Sunday did I write
For the neighborhood
for
A heaven before tomorrow.

Northern Dawn

Frost upon the window in the morning
Foghorns mark the break of day
Between such moments lies a sorrow
Fearing the day could blow away

What good is last night's pleasure gone?
What good's today when blown astray?
All the currents are the play
Occurrences aren't sewn to stay.

Buzzbudblinkbo

Buzzbudblinkbo
seated on a picture show
dimensional as come and go
blow the man down lassie,

beebopblind amo
caught up to the granny
stuck in luck newcomer was struck
after ever went the moon

goosegrease jumbo
cat licked cotton
same one next time
soon forgotten

somebitch dirty pearly held
up the end blasted faith less
taking on celibate trust for teens
moving eagerly

all on along watchtower heads
looking back remembering shared beds
nifty new old worlds forging on blarny, rolling
stones in infant snow lost age before begun

and the tyrant was a teeniewhiner raised
on petty suffering
the outcome was a victim of a wholesome fellow
there were no justice, artifice or cockatoo
dawn alarms
to set the precipice of recipee

came along off went in through the out door

didn't mind the rules ran a red into a ford

called a commie labor buster beckoned on a holy shit

taken back for beating fine tune to discover what to knit

when in fact the dawning day was far away

why? because in truth there were more games to play

but that was nellyaftersinging sourly disease

a trifle pilgrimage unto the dark horse

a storybook remembrance of a dim course

illuminated by a hookydoo

skidding through the frosting woods

looking out for manger doers.

Questions on The Banks of the Mississippi

Is there more?
                    Is there less?
Let us take some time to guess
Let us roam the riverbanks and get our souls undressed
            Unleash our fears and paranoia's
 frustrations and remorse
Let them run free through the forest
 to leave ourselves a peaceful stroll

Need we more? Need we less?
Must we slave or shall we rest?
Is their conquest in our stride?
Shall we walk while we can ride?
Do we have or need a vision?
Does some master hold the clue?
Are we tame or are we viscous?
                    Come, let's heed the river
                            Watch it flow, see what it grows

Are we more? Are we less?
Than insects killed as pests
Are we ourselves or are we driven?
Do we know our mother Earth?
Dare we hate? dare we love?

Disobedient the tide
                    Full of passion, ***burst the damn!***
I hear a distant thunder say,

I cleanse myself of what dismay
May be dissolved,
dismantled

I sense my soul to the well returning
 to the coldness of the Earth, I succumb
After ascending heights, flights of ecstacy
 Down into a tomb to feed
The mighty river of time perpetual

Be we more, be we less
 Be we better hosts and guests
Upon the tidings of our times, we ride
          the crescent waves of fortune
Stolen away from future days
 To a past irreverent, unweighed.

Lake Phoebe, August

The many euphoric moments
hazeled between our glorious dreams
send me swirling, with but a glimpse of the depth
of eternity

Eternally,
boast and swagger the sublime
while infantile the divine
an echo in a still moist forest
softly wavering

A devil waits with cure and potion
as harmony,
circles round a raindrop on the pond
spreading what has been uttered
while
tearful, soft, some feel the trees
whisper as they dance so unencumbered.

Back Where No Path Goes

Back where no path goes
Everything grows
where the white birch lie
the caterpillar wrestles
attacked and carried away by an army
of ants as mosquitos
buzz in the air
up from the dew, beneath the moon
As a loon sings of the cosmos

wildflowers, moss and pine brush
grow
  thick
diverse

While lies from the inside of our worlds
rapidly transform

ripples form around raindrops in a giant mirror
  cool, fresh and deep

masquerade off
  a pioneer again

discovering
our forgotten origin
unsynthesized, unprogrammed
 uneducated, knowing nothing
as the wind commands the trees into a symphony
back where no path goes

everything grows.

Riding the Careless Tide to the Shore

I was going to curse about economic despair
when I caught a breath
of air
A world much bigger than our own
                                        Faintly
imaginable
indigestible, magnificent

I was watching sludge pouring into the river
Counting the broken glass
 waste paper, bicycle parts, used oil
   fast food containers, styrofoam, cans and plastic
And I was going to shed a tear
for the Natives
choking on booze and exhaust

But instead I caught a promise
poking through my raw inside
as I bent down to pick up the shit washed in by the
careless tide
I felt a shiver
of death for those riding silent
on that tide
          caressing none, thoughtlessly killing generations to
come

Out in the wilderness
 reality calls
    The North wind blows
Last night Northern Lights filled the sky and my mind
was ablaze with enchantment
drug free, natural
Now a dragonfly
lands on me staring, cocking its head
checking me out and I it
wondering
why

there is no merit, value or reward
issued for
this moment

Twisted the ways
Never clarifying the haze
Between gumdrop glitter
And born anew chatter
Then hustle up bargain
Employment for sale
And rushed, the brain
Falls to escaping

Bring spring water for the city man
Cool, fresh water
For him to feast his complicated thoughts on
As never will answers come completed
Neither will his extension end

Of all the katydid dreamfests
That weave the grand quilt: Eternity
Which belongs to an unamplified voice?

a silent whisper coloring the dark
without applause, fanfare or critique
Trivial finale of physical comprehension
a world dies with each

                                    a world grows to
teach

Bring fresh water for the city man
Heavy platforms cannot balance peace
   humor and birdsinging ease
The cold, shiny calculable machine
 grinding up nature to suit its needs.

Time

time

  T I M E

t   i   m   e

escaping again, It can't be caught
Life's a perpetual race with the clock
and you can't quit, No
Not unless you've found
a niche, an
original way to get independently rich
Time **tick** tock time **tick** time tick clock **beep**
Arise to alarm and get with the news
Plug into coffee and keep lit that fuse running
through the day Quick Hurry there just ain't enough
hours in the day to get it all done, life is
short, life is empty, don't forget to
get all the bills paid and keep
up with the neighbors, get laid, drunk escape
it's all you can do, they've got
clocks in the bars, in the gardens, on the wrist
strapped to the clock, beep, it keeps the heart beating, tick
Heart attack fast life, fast food, thrills
satisfaction immediate or why bother at all
patience old fashioned, the wait, pre-technology
Go baby go son brother don't slow
cruise climb the mountain be the king, you're squire is
time
tick tock

well,
I've seen em run crazy in New York City
I've felt my soul drained by this insane pace
A reluctant contender in most every race, I don't care
I'd rather be
a steadfast tree.

By a Bright Clear Morning Stream

To watch the birches, twisted, stand
 Against a sky of unscarred blue,
Spotlighted by twinkling beams up from
 a casually rapid passing stream,

Relates to me a connection
 deeper than fad philosophy
true as the root grasping the soil
 dynamic, in relation
dearer than the course
 of machines turning clockwise
churning dustless corridors of fate
 corroding away
   tomorrows

Rocks and soil painted with afternoon shadows
 leap to me and call,
and no longer will I crawl
 face to the mopping up floor

when a heart leaps to saddle the breeze
 warmed by delicate fortune
purely natural and free
 I'll leap with thee.

Testament

Here I drink, There I will sleep
And he who weeps on my shoulder I'll hold
We shall fly, my brother and I
nose in the earth dirt, feeling the thunder
Speeding through classy chrome scenes
We as a team shall nourish
Beyond brilliance, sweat for an ounce
of gestures unsung but oh the nobility
Poetically wailing at unjust worlds
as inside calming treasures of peace fulfill
where once, waning wilted alone
The full moon shone guilty and cheated

So insignificant, alive and reviving
Colors from cobwebs merge to create
Life in pursuit, stagnant without love
Lonely highway in a rich automotive
Invisible
to the wonderment
of roadsides blooming
with exits and detours to unimagined destinies
Every arrival a masterpiece
Every dismissal is death

Fear no more the reaper
Greed and conformity the demon
Sure as blood flows from lover to stranger
Through the mirror I see poverty
A small planet trembles

Forever tolls the fatal bell
Bones washed upon the shore
An empire not everlasting
Minor contributors at best aren't we?
dancing on arrogance, Living in luxury
Modern day
Wholly impudent
Might ask if you were lost?
Will we ever stand to change?

Ageless injustice, silly poet
Report beauty, reap glories
Ripped apart by world news

Humankind waning, come together
Fight no more battle minds
Cherished ethnicity and pride
As a whole may we rise
Against the probability of
 eternal war

Buried nearly in the flight
If I see I will cast
When I cease
I'll be dust

I strain my hands for the unborn
To be a saint, yet human do I fall
So frequently in shallow water

The hour alive, come hither
All ye questioning, lost in pursuit
My end is your beginning
I, not mute can only tell
The tale of what I feel.

**A glass of water
From a cool pitcher
With ice cubes**

Purity
From the planet obscured
by manufactured soda

I Read The News Today, Oh Boy!

America keeps getting richer
As America is getting poor
As the Exxon Valdez spills
Ten thousand gallons in pristine Prince William Sound
So many cry
To stamp out the big business villain
But who, I ask
Backs up their cry by cutting their
dependance on
that oil?

America gets richer
As America gets poorer
As new models hit and leave the auto showroom
Freeways congest and jam
and nobody moves very fast
Exhaust stinks up to the ozone,
But immune inside our own vehicles, secluded travelling
One ear on the cell phone
Air conditioned, to the frequency of choice
Honking
For others to get out of our way

America
Is getting richer
Corporate mergers, the wealth is growing
Cities springing upwards, magnificent towers
But there's no one to pay the rent
and America goes into debt

And the neighbors think themselves poor
They can't afford
The latest model car to jam the freeway
Like the Jones' and the Johnsons
next door who keep
Building their house bigger
It's not a question of greed
There's food and shelter, met are needs

But void of luxuries there's no redemption
No success
America is getting poorer
Technology
is taking over
American's are just too valuable
To employ
At twelve bucks an hour
too drastic a cut
in lifestyle might
cut too much on production
wrecking the economy, saving the forest
  rivers and air
so raped and polluted
let the third world produce
so America consumes
Let technology work
While America lounges
immune
In it's burning tepee

Ask the true American's
The few surviving natives
if
America is getting rich or poor?
Ask them if they need the oil
Ask them when they got their booze?
Ask them why they
Haven't got with the game and raced
highly motivated through the workweek to
the new car showroom.
Ask them why they
don't want suburbia
won't cut their hair
won't bear the cross, after all
father white man must know best

For history favors the conqueror, victor
History is written by
The winner.

History follows the beast
Glorifying bestiality
I learned it in grade school
About the pirates, raping and killing
In the name of
Freedom, God and other greeds
The white man
is getting
richer

Stereo's are better
Television's are bigger, brighter, to better define
reality

10.1 million gallons spilled
119 dead sea otters
hundreds of dead birds
And it's only Tuesday
Congress has yet to vote
On a bill to approve oil drilling
In the Arctic National Wildlife Refuge

Merry Christmas Little Ones

Merry Christmas little ones
Mercy sakes we've lots of guns
Maybe someday we'll be more
Like Christmas that we all adore

Crime corrodes away the throne
Destroys a humble Christmas home
Christening the killing clone

Christmas comes too soon
Or is it soon enough?
Shops are full but shallow is the hope, forever fighting
Music interrupted by the news
Replacing horridly the carols
Madness reigning overhead
What can we people do to show
The world we'd like it not to blow
up?

Blank faces wander
        I wonder if they care
Night now lasts longer
                I wonder if I dare
        Steal out in winter cold
        To act not loud or bold
                Only to behold
the tragic terror, magic treasure
Life

Penny heads on down to the saloon before
  the clock strikes noon
Andy goes to work to earn a penny not a richer life
Though the sun may brightly burn
A few hung in the mist do yearn
somewhere for the hope to help
before the world melts
What can we people do?

Soon we people will be through
Christmas presents are but toys
Christmas bells ring lots of noise
Bringing magic to the world and joys
Packed away in cardboard boxes
 and stored stiff in the attic

The Christmas craze will come and go
The rest left for a routine show
Will we people ever show
Desire for a world we'd like to know?

Merry Christmas little ones
Mercy sakes we've lots of guns
Maybe someday we'll be more
Like Christmas that we all adore.

Father Flintstone

Black except for collar, Father Flinstone passes
across the quiet monastery, cane in hand
Poor old man
All sensation sacrificed for faith in the unearthly
A lofty love, I'd think such lonely nights
Can you really lift mankind?

Giving birth to hypocrites and
martyrs
May a good lord strike me
down for I
Look no more to the sky for
answers
I seek truth in the eyes of those
Who walk among the Earth at home

Your polished shoes on the lain stone path
Father see these seasons pass
Pacing back and forth awaiting
Entry to another world.

The Holy Grail

So many souls
In need of healing
Stubbornly refusing
Admission into
heaven,

When the fact is
We've been here all along
It's just hard to find
Bulldozed, while racing to clocks
That don't even need winding
anymore

Perpetually ticking
Building, flying in airplanes
Consuming, erasing
yesterday
And losing today in the race

Losing touch with any base
Spineless, formless
Given to the whim of a moment
A media suggestion, a Snicker's bar
Sugar, caffeine, sneed and liquor
                                    removed
right now as I sit
Meditating on a fallen tree
Letting hours pass
to ease and relax
My mind so clouded
with the abstract.

Genesis

In some proverb
was it written
peace be to the
highest people

and There's gotta be
A zillion secret
poets in this
evolving
gateway

Spreading seeds about
to sprout

Laying burdens down
for soul

Someday will the garden span the globe?
(Was it
so long ago
that poetry was king

of my soul?

Were it only
passing waves
towards metropolis shore?

Upon heaven's door
I knock and heed
the warning and the greeting
arms open wide, relating
common ground

the small steps, as passengers
upon eternity we take)

Should our sentence trace
Our lives into the flames
Of raging alien desire?
Or might the manufactured
abstracted misdirection
point the way to mechanical being?
Might we stoke or cool the fire?
air conditioned, genetically bred

                        please,
              Connect with some blade of grass
                                    you walk on

Builder of factories and shopping malls

        Our heavy human steps cannot be light enough

                    the deluge and the petty wars
                          devouring
                                    humanities
                                    and Earth

is nature only birth?

Z O O M !

Caves and fire
Club and claw
Electric blanket
Nuclear bomb

ZOOM!
Airplanes across the bright blue sky
On a waterbed two lovers lie
In a slaughterhouse cows line up
Mice caged in a laboratory
To cure disease so we live with ease
Dividing the world up by east and west walls
Falls a space capsule right into the sea
Underneath submarines are always on guard
Prepared to ignite nuclear bombs
While boys in fast cars are cruisin downtown
Picking up girls wearing make-up like clowns
Blasting loud stereos **Rock'n Roll**
Reigns the wild beat of our young fast feet
Heat from the fireplace furnace

microwave
Skyscrapers reaching
Up lakes getting cleaned back

Up
Factories swiftly packing freeze dried goods
In a can in a can
All you need to eat is an opener
And no good sense
Airplanes cigarettes
Credit cards and

discotheques
Television toilets flushing
Telephones and bathtub

toys
Cement jungles multilingual
Pocket size computers
Nine to five commuters ride the train runs beneath the bay
Video arcades, for a quarter you can join a fad

Dye your hair green be a punk
Blast in Headphones electronic funk
Call coast to coast and touch someone
Across the world on the TELEphone
Call a taxi it'll get you there
Brightly colored underwear!
Women wearing nothing radiated by the swimming pool
Cocaine up your nostrils grilling wieners on the barbecue
X-rays from the doctor, laser beam routine
Plastic plates stainless steel
Manufactured in Hong Kong

Nothing lasts that long, disposable
Marriage down the drain, removable
Artificial stimulants insemination aggravation
Lost in static communication
So many toys not time to try
Electric lights replace the moon
Phone answering machines leave no one home while
The television screen
SCREAMS
Indians are fought off by the cavalry
Interrupted by an add for jello

Chairlifts to the mountaintop
To slalom down in stylish clothes
Facelifts for the masses
Who don't know how
Nasty habits multiply
How good they have it
Food and drink * Drugs video
Architects drawing cities
In the sea and on the moon
Spoon fed fat kids
Starving third world orphans
Preachers in their pulpits
Couples in the bushes
Cruising speedy freeways on a lazy smoggy afternoon
Drinking in a tavern on a starry neon night

Landed on the moon more than ten years ago
Heart attacks and cancer plague the young and old
Stadium rock concerts -- lotta drugs
Tailgating football -- lots of booze
Every morning waking drinking lots of java
Racing down the highways at the reckless speed of
Skyrockets
Pickpockets
Kidnappers
Panhandlers
Terrorists tease
Soldiers seize
I hear it on the news
Luxury airliners crash
Hundreds killed at once
Factory hardworking veterans
Replaced by machines
Beggars in the streets
Baby cries of hunger
Man rapes baby's mother
Elevators escalators
Politicians promise more
No trust among
People crying more for peace
Screaming for a nuclear **FREEZE**
Picture postcards
Microchips
Computer graphics
Paper clip
Round and fat our world is
Richly full of this and that
Eating piece by piece I'm
Glad I wish I could eat faster
But I can't eat any faster
Or I wouldn't taste at all
I must maintain a sane pace
To sustain a piece of

peace

Anything well packaged sells
Junkyards smell
  Water skiis to walk on water
  Bullet trains and toilet paper
   Factory rot and smoke and stench
    Noise and lies and fine perfume
    What is there we can't do?
                     Paper wrapped fast food
             Smaller grows the world
      Larger bursts the cities and the suburbs
               What is there we can't do?
         Caves to highrises
        Wheel to jet skies
     What is there we can't
                  do?

What?

      What?
             What?

  What?
         What?
           `What?

     What?
         What?
      What?

             What?

     What?
         What?

What?

nature is not for cardboard boxes

gottagr
oove

starta
fuse

lesseningcon
fusion

sucker atethe
dust

  Lightning made delusion
  Soon became
obsession
       Put it all
              behind
                   Ride the Tide!
  on ahead
        of way hey

      mister can you spare a rib or two?

           Great o'seer of waves
        Crashing poetics on the shore
        Uncapturable
          eternity
               Contaminated

Rise we through our fresh breath back to Eden
               resources distributed Humane
seeping in global and cosmic relation
        the runway to heaven replaced
man,
you can soar it right on out of this world
Fade to black.

                    or Up with the houselights!
                        let the sun shine
                        warm your ledger and spine
no electric neon
impulses true,

Pulses of energy
 syncopating daydream
 locking into history
                                Truth is divine
Beauty blooms, recognized
                        each moment weightless
Until the inevitable landing
 burdened cry, Existence
                Rationale to   isolate
 daisies grass and wind chimes singing
                        Eternal riddles for brain teased
        mortals
Trying to race by
mortality
 unaware that
        life races away

Unveil the flower!
                Exhibit the dew
Cliffs of Big Sur beneath a full moon
                        Visions of fine everafters
        Bedding with cynical crashes
                Who is the woman? Who is the man?
        Subservient roles to Earth heaven

Infinity, texture
Sky is the space
mind dwelling place
 outward from the center
Grow long your beard Adam
        Grow long your hair Eve
Nature is not for cardboard boxes.

Organic Kaleidoscope

Bathed in all creation
Let the winds of eternity howl
I, with my beast, am at home on the globe
  with the madness and nonsense spinning

Deeper in progress, in moist green, in hue
Reckless the cobweb that has spun the dew
Safer, yet setback, the shadow asks, mentioning
of his master the sun, looming like
 a frank kaleidoscope wisdom
Feeding a nest of dancing sunbeams
 upon a port of wind tossed waves

Cruising through the dew, creation always new
humbler than goat herders high up on the Alps
here with my eternal, fragile china cup
there with a splash, a cloud scar on the sky
so effervescent, in ecstacy am I
  truly
 in this hour of our happy escapade

Oh wisdom, what end
        What nonsense and hollow
How to shake you to move
        your heart to follow truth

That path layeth bare as you outgrow your youth
        Cement over the orchard and wild grass, where
in this concrete and steel and microchip
  went your soul?

Quivering with the genius in all common fabric
Intertwined with a glimpse of mere insects and moss
Alive! Beyond convention of toxic flatulence
 Beyond the dust blown wide from the sneer
Beyond the miracle of creation we've been
  invited to cook, ourselves in the pot

Tossed out to the meadow to bloom, oh
                    Sweet symphony arise!
Song of the loon! Thunder snare the heavens!
            Crash the beaver's enterprise
Catch my heart panting, breathless
             vultures swirling overhead for dear-
                ly the recipe
has a place for all
eternity

Let those winds of eternity howl to me
 Cleansed of soul destruction, I alas am free
wanton and frugal, logentivity's potion
No secrets to hide, a jubilee be shared
All is celebration
The joy
of creation
toil
 and burden
Sweet sweat and pain
A bloodstained hour glass
eager
as every hour approaches.

beside a woman sleeping

Who is she
beside me now
breathing
softly, somewhere
afar
in a dream
like myself

It's frightening, so
Disguising
Hard to believe it's
even real

the Past done, swallowed
Commercialized
Jingle, jangle

Spaces to fall
drift
in emptiness
despair
to fill
with infinitely rich
harmony

Windows
Roads and bridges
documents of earnest lines
built upon
Sunshine between those lies
Whispered to ease
Tears

Who is she beside me now
asleep as I wander
the hollow fortress of my infinite dreams?

how do you sleep?
with restless schemes as I
impatient to shed my disguise and shine true
for all of the world to bruise, i need
you to love
to forget myself
to fade my cursing
i need
someone to believe in and to hold
to nourish and to boldly
love where lovers have not loved before
spreading love about the streets and crevices
giving hope to the unloved, and birth yet to the dead

oh how easy and so deep
it seems all the world's asleep, just carrying on

sweep me off my destiny again
lift my soul out of the grave
a scent of life, a touch so tender
awakened to fatherhood, a beggar

        warm sigh of ecstasy
        beneath the wrinkled fabric
        of folded ambitions wrestled and tossed
away
        to glorious dawns
                    Adieu dreams of destiny!
                      here now am I
beside me is she
yet a mystery filling me
with a bursting sense
of unfathomable joy

where are you now, I await
more of your magic to intoxicate
me, it's
happiness like this for the whole world
 that I long
to greet.

Exit Existentialism

Brain arranged heaven
hear the call of the Earth
under a spell of remoteness
the convention a curse

open the lid, dawn precedes alarm
Take free your aim, come clear the stream
Lay down righteous arms, grow your enterprise larger
 than the curious wit of a conceited dream

what shall remember, cleared the plain
again the dawn has bathed its game
commence the stirrup and the dance
 naked in the wilderness, time has won
as lightning strikes, the mighty
 rots into the ground

it all grows on each other
a harmony so complete, it calls
to no one.

From Prairie to the Sea

Afternoon melodic, silent
Herds of clouds majestic, roam
None betrayed, no promise made
No foundation lain
A perfect lair
in the weaving

dutiful
In the breaking
of waves
fresh, aghast
inspecting clover
significant and worldly

Wide, sacred realm
the interconnectedness
of bliss
strolling
home to the prairie where
once the buffalo did
roam,

Did glow
On the horizon
Sweet, fantastic settling
Of harmony bred
by Earth's abundant superette
Acting as a garden
To leap into faith, dwelling
Adolescents on the shore
tying into more
day glowing scenes of heaven lore
fantastic
abstract, becoming
by the hammer and the hand unglued
proportions
of inexhaustible rebirth

Magnificent decay
rotting and toil and wonder
amidst all, wonder
wandering to the brook, to find
where the foundation of life lies

Herds keep rolling
Overhead
Daring to lay waste
the enterprise

Entertaining
open minds bewildered
by cosmic
correlations

Radiated
Possoming
Near and murky
Water clapping
    forest whispers
ripples, spines across
the equinox

of fate
 and desire to be
again

a
footbridge to
The other side
Where lovers meet at moonlight to
Sail the tide
Of fantasy
Caressing
Quintessentially

        Gunshots break the silence
Crowing righteous and defiant
        Rowboats tied up to the pier
Poetry, so fragile, near

No boundaries, no molds
Elevate a cosmic whole
        Before the strong winds of eternity
Vast and vegetationless
        Elevate a cosmic whole
No boundaries, no molds
        One universe, inside and out
Where do I walk the plank?
        No killing ever life creating
Thirst in always ever land, I
Ask once more if the shore isn't lore
If it's only temporary and I'm only dreaming
Tide breaking, revelation
Unfiltered sun fries my flesh

        Earth
     Vast ocean
Shouting ocean, fathomless note
I see sky above art's clouds
My shouts are drowned
My shirt balloons
Darkening sea, aloof am I
   Speak you to me?

And the sea cried back
 An illogical song
Blew back the tease
 That had haunted so long
Gave credence to spirit
 Giving birth yet to hope

Someday a politic fool will o'ertake me
        Or so says history
A just man peaceful, ner prevails
        Persuasion twists a lovers passion

Little sanderling, I'm wondering
Deeds of so many obscured
The sea washes back the absurd
Bullwhip and driftwood
Shark leftovers, shells --
Time caressed smooth, ancient
Oh sea,
Take me out with your tide
As you whisper

Stranded tide pools
Insects swarm the feast
Scavengers eat sand for the crabs
After the high tide deserts

Man made his wings to hang with the birds over
Ocean is life is an ocean
Divideless
Uncatagorizeable
Employed in leisure
Life is an ocean is life
Reservoir of the Earth ball
Cleanser and spirit
Persuasionless teacher
Who speaketh to me
As I walk in the sand
Leaving tracks to be washed
Away.

traveling

Brain bleeding morsels of obsolete art
Taking a breath of for granted air
Faint breath fading away

                                        is it real?
What is this strange sound of the sea?
I came to write some poetry
 but everything is instant

Nor are these scenes eternal
I'm camping out

amidst redwoods, standing proud

no artifice or stimulants obscuring
this beauty pure

filling me with so few needs
& words
that I am at last reborn

delivered from life in denial
freedom floats a sweet scent on the breeze
my burdens I have found amidst the trees

Of this metal trash can I'm aware
Chained into the ground
I'm aware
Of a burned out picnic grill

                                The thrill
                                of diving deep
Native of another plane
Humanity, the stranger
Destinations are but castles in the clouds,
Remedies to ease the pain
It's thrilling just to get you there
The journey is
those scenes eternal
this reality
 We're passing through.

awaiting moonbeams

awaiting moonbeams
standing steadfast on a rock
on a summer night
by a tranquil lake

breath stirred, aghast
is true at peace, a laugh?

Swimming With The Loons at Sunset

A symphony of loons
swimming in the sunset
invite me to a dip

As twists the misbegotten sinews
Deepened in a still pool
Beside which the body cools, stills

and peace is lurking
suddenly

A perfect, true attainment

Suddenly

time has stopped

frequent dilemmas satisfied
heaven tribe

stillness

Reality Transformation

The day affords, caring for all
Today alone, no clocks meddling
sail clouds and dance the waters
as echoing
creatures call against the wind

Answer no pratfalls or downtrodden curse
heaven is lathed with righteous fervor
even in hate, is truth a shimmer
arranges the darkness, a benevolent saint

Look everywhere, hope is around you
The planet will endure
Humanity so lofty, but an ant
dwelling in its beehive sphere
Nature compensates for all

Modern society, steadfast and bold
Here I sit, undeserved
About to hatch, unglued to the seam
Stream flows and forest grows
It all comes into me now,

The freshness, the aroma
Lakes of life inspire me new
Tis not for thee that I have sunken
I conform now to the trees
Mists of wonder, soft clapping waves
Preserved, unpolluted land
ancient and tall
when we kill, we fall
survival of the fittest
means death
to a humanity capable
of enhancing
planetary
harmony

Do I believe in harmony, I believe
entrusted are fools
so beautifully conceived, they're doomed
to dare let heaven take them in
the heaven in our minds
When our heaven is the earth

Born here on this Earth
We are of the Earth
We are with the hawks and fish
Creatures of the Earth

Great and small, We take to flight
fight in war Pollute our home
 as well the beaver
        Falls a tree
As well I tell this tale for thee

Eternity, untouched, uncursed
It matters not that we are of the earth
Except to Mother Earth
And so we fill our dreams
With personas of the bold, proud human race
And what we lay to waste is only private epitaphs
 no kings of all creation after all
  heaven in our minds, we carry on
bricks and steel and currency grow
Spirits no lesser nor greater than
a steadfast moose caught grazing
in a stream at sunset

It all comes into me now
World of wonder, refreshed, anew
I conform no longer to
a paranoid, polluted land.

Looking Deeply in the Night

When I look into this night
I see all is ordinary and I'm bored
Wanna run atop it all
I'm a young man, I won't fall
Wanna hug the moon but it's too far away
Wanna race my car across infinity
                              But it won't start

Then again I look into the night
And everything's alright
My uptight lullabies are foolish
As is my delight

All that really matters is
the ground we walk, the air we breath
The life we feed

Bring on the night
Let sad hearts drool
Sadness merely an organic tool
Power and might but a tease to desire
Which mold human souls
Hearts burn dry in the fire

What humankind
Conceives in the mind
So much, far to travel
Unknown islands in ourselves
Remaining foreign and unnoticed
Muscle getting scarce
mind growing strong
An equal balance must we reach
To make the melody of life eternal
from a song

When I look into this night
 I know everything's alright
Nothing's so important
Jewels are not valuable
The world is not cruel

Stars beam so elegant

The night sky rules.

Caught in a Storm and Shipwrecked

More dreaming, set the course straight
 An arrow to the heart and mind
Soars overhead, an eagle
  Drifting on the breeze against the drama of the sky
Travelling on the tide, my canoe swiftly
  passes on by

Storm clouds tumble across the hilltops
Sharply, the wind takes grasp
Catching me motionless, reflecting
 on a myriad of patterns on the water
  suddenly achieving depth, force

Then the fires roar and levitate
the water, heaven's greeting has been sent
In deepest dismay and furthest astray
Community passes, an isle in the storm
  beseeched, terrors, infinity screams
Crashing from the sky, God's hammer comes scolding
Alone in a vortex, a mortal
  swirling,

Captain, the frightening winds
Took control, beyond legion and measure
Sound fury dissected, an insignificant being
Sustained 'neath the thundering, the flowering strong

Stricken life, death,
harmony, violence
On Earth, beyond reach of machine
 in the forest
Who rides this ship, who coined the pen?
Run off the depths and back from hell again
To dry with the stiffening afternoon breeze
Ripening in an August sun, dreams of moon-
 child far beyond
the sinews twisting
 a hearth, a breast
Quivering

as insects swarm to occupy
the night

Uncaring of the dangers
inherent
in being

distrustful of the obvious and known
heaven is endowed
with wary passengers
of the deluge.

      draw me out
long dead lore, forgotten visions
bequeathed with harmony, armed
with knowledge of despair, and wondrous invitations
into a fool's
heaven
I bequeath
my misfortune on the deserved
A pasteur for the crown

to Grow beyond an age of destruction
Lead us bold technology to understanding
   to
        Love the organic, incomprehensible
        The rocks, the grass, the seas
The tantalizing breeze

The creatures we exist with
 birds and fish and insects
  the plants, the trees
     majestic seas
clouds above, the rain, the soil
All Mother Earth, her growth and spoils
     Infinity unfathomable
      as we the meek
        create a wake
        trying to find our way out
           of the black hole in space
and inside our souls

Peace to your neighbor, peace to your brother
Peace to your enemy and oppressor too
Peace may flow
through me and you
Connecting us
To no longer shade our darkness from the sun
If our souls are pure
 are desires are one
and we the impenetrable
shall with the creatures of heaven, exist

All the peoples of the Earth
All the animals and birds
Every tree and flower precious
All life a unique entity
Together meshed in harmony

As I lye on my lifebed
I fear the end and feel the dawn
The simplest acts of love shine
No greater feat unto humankind
Burden that anchors down the soul
Is lifted, into marriage
Humanity weds nature and upgrades
It's home, planet of abundance
Let poor be fed, let life enrich
Materialism, eclipsed by pureness wanes
Each individual standing in tune
Uniquely
Without threatening the harmony

harmony

Sacred Mother of us all
Beyond the here and now are cries
Our noblest strides are for the children.

and on...

Starting out
Into the strange depths of the night
I heard an owl
beneath a gull cry
and then a howl
unlike any earthly sigh
that startled my mind into a wisdom
more sound than any fragile system

So quickly diffused and forgetting
Losing track of where I am
What place, what time, with whom?

Surfing off to the cerebral sea
Confused amidst the chaos
of humanity,

Motion sickness, speedbumps racing
Blind and bold, trampling, spending
Consuming without paying back
Conforming to the toys

Truth reigns only in the moment
Experience crystallizes into fiction
Life is elsewhere, life is for
  the beholder

in tune amidst
the muse

Blizzard

White sky falling
Thick flakes in currents dance
Drifts flare up and disappear
Horizon brushed away

Ah snow, wonderful snow
Falling, falling
Where do we go from here?

Blows the wicked wind
Soon I shan't be watching
Roams a restless kid
So short is the storm

Ghosts tap on the window
Racing by and begging
Begging to get in
Swelling sores of howling winds
Spinning whirlpool, ground exploding
Violent cold
Falling, freezing
Where do we go from here?

So small, so tiny
Darkness closes the curtain
Stealing, invading
No respect for the dying
Fearful pines are shivering
Ah snow, wonderful snow
Pure and frightening symphony
Heavy icy blanket
Steady the stance and braid the ambition
Calling, crawling
Play your music and light a fire
Burning, glowing
None of it comes from above except the
Snow, wonderful snow
Falling.

epitaph

a stone makes circles in the water

life encompasses

the weighted soul

patterning after it submerges

and dissolving

into ripples with the wind.

A Buskin For The Frump

The Way of Love

Rain falling on the freeway
Steam covers the windows

Wipers, rhythm --
for a moment in sync
with music on the radio,

and isn't that the way of love?

A moment later
out of sync again.

Man Checks Watch, Swiftly
*(Striding Towards The Car After One Cup Of Joe, Coat
Flapping In The Wind)*

It seems so much is swallowed up
In a consciousness aloof, plucked
    and dropped
    into destiny by an obsolete machine,

Recognizing
in the mirror a struggling yupster
    Too little time, too little cash
        to make a dash for riper ground while living
    on the make,

 And yet
the past and future wake
        on the doorstep every morn
            A fiddler enticing a dance with the wind
    Out
        across this mote of comfort, casting
                                dignity away

 Or is it
more
of the rigged score
            ? tied up, more tv, IV fed
                                            up

nearly,
 meaning to call up a few of the famous
hip hardy pranksters
Nearly,
 needing a God to rid landfills of Pampers
Near sacrificing all the holiness of life for
the elusive,
  imprisoning,
  planet raping

American Dream.

Maynard C. Blues

Monday morning hung
up on the freeway boxed into traffic
trying to jive on the radio jam
trying to get with the program still while my mind, scarred
hears birds, serenading
mundane science with their harmony, transporting me
Inside a memory, I feel again
  that fresh spraying waterfall far
from civil
 -ization, I'm
the first to admit,
Peace don't permeate my outward stroll
but I know there's a whole
helluva lotta doom
round the corner, if we don't
sew some seeds
real, like, soon.

Fossiling out, feeling
what ulcers are made of, I've been
before bludgeoned, tight in a grip, life weighed down
I've hung strange ideals and wept at the moon
Stacking old books and selling new toys
Until morning's just noise
Hot ego steam, belligerent reigns
warm showers, unconcerned
        about the water, hung
Waitin' on inspiration, trying
  to focus beyond
 the kaboomblingmetropolis as breezes sway west,
then right and back left
and then in a damned dizzying whirlpool I'm stranded
laughing at arrogance and death
            chattering with reincarnations of birth
                    A return to the brink, while a lie
runs
the purpose contrived,

Waves of immortal destiny drive
fueling the unknown,
truth bruises and blooms in a dreamlike state,
endlessly brought down.

I should have known better than to mingle
with pleasant pretty folk
speaking in calm tones of the weather
while cheering teams to smother
eden with strange dreams of Heaven
"Ain't no problem's here in God's country.
Monday morning's strait and perfect, No
goblins for the heaven sent,"
Slashing at the pagan's tent
in puddles of blood boiling fervor, splashing
Back from the war victorious and gory, cuttin'
down the forests now to make
a profit so that we can all die rich, so
our babies can grow up to live

                                               off toxic wasted
streams,
seems
 daylight suffers intolerable schemes
nothing is quite as we ought to believe
and we're going down,
down

over the jagged summit
down
Spilling huge
shitloads of oil
secreting
radioactive diseases
belching
flatulence up through the ozone
Monday morning's
hung,

man,

idling engines reek
business interests falsely speaking
I turn the dial on the radio but anyway I tune it
Monday's hung
barely
eaking
out a living

and sweeping consciousness under the rug.

Put In Irons

I.

young man, grand dreams
moonbeams

stone baggage, taxed knowledge
forced routine

inviable
villianless
willing

II.

Irons in the fire get destroyed
unattended, dreaming rainbows and ripe green pastures of
someday

A world away, old memories stir
Forging on dawns like tractor treads
  Bulldozing right over the spring
as
carefree 'neath the sun
 play the young, calling
my heart to beat strong, amiss

as I feel the tug tighten like a noose round the neck
a bottle of luxury seeming too much for the present, put off
by fossilized remains of squires
dying with irons in the fire.

III.

        We
knew well
    the smell
of afternoons given away
to concrete insanity, It was a given

that marching in line was makin' a living.

Being

Breezes, Jesus!
      How time goes by
Idly in comfort as airline engines fly
Overhead roaring vibrations of grand eloquent adventures,
Sure I've got a map of Europe dotted with some precious tales.

                If only
           One could turn back the clock and do it
      Again and again forever, never
Having to part with old lovers and friends . . .

                       Sweeping cobwebs from this room,
ticking
             with shadows crawling along the wall
                     houseplants growing tall
             roots deepening, holding down the
tumbleweed, the
           outrageous whimsy and carefree abandonment

      There's no looking back,
Shadows don't halt
          Twirls not the horizon but our foundation
                     in space, Is time

      a dimension for humbling
   the boisterous claims of rebellion and change?

Jesus, breezes!
How time goes by,
Enriching soil with rain
Mixing pleasure and pain
Never sure of the stance, its
  a cowardly pose, holding
Onto the towing rope, serving
while
Maneuvering

to the port of eternity

                    accepting
        slower lanes and sober dawns
as
monuments stand tall but false
when

None commands like the gentle breeze,
  buds of spring release rebirth.

And out of such stale indoor amusement
  wanders the old, intellectual sage
Receiving a ceaseless echo of the same tough questions
  now unasked, still unanswered
As unchained plots grow farther from reach;

Removing heavy worn shoes and strolling
barefoot in emerging grass
with gratitude, to be here still
unfilled
only by abstracted standards, devouring
appreciation
of the simple beauty of merely
being.

The Mediocrity of Modern Life

If the mechanic don't get ya, the bankers will
When you're poor, they're gonna keep you down
Eighteen bucks for this, for that
Sixteen more for tit and quack
seven for
an ounce, a buzz
panhandled out on the auto lot,

Stuck in the mold, balancing
hungover on the manifold, directionless
conventionist
plugging packaged pasta on a prime time rerun
nudging forth notions of a heavenly armada
  sailing into eden 'fore the taxman taketh
all those rainy dreaming days away,

                    Gesturing convention
                    for the memory of satisfaction
                    Cosmic fella falls
                    down the Man-hole, tripping in solvents
foamy water, bubbling Lawrence Welk texture to a crystal
                    clear mood that won't comply
                    with work-a-day logic,

        If the insurance don't get ya, the utilities will
        To keep it'll cost ya, to keep warm it'll break you
        to keep fire in the soul and belly well,
        a marvelous abstract anecdotal placebo paid for by your
        generous taxes is gonna steal the mic from your homeless
        plight call it *"A thousand points of light."*

Perhaps the moon knows what it's like to be fascinating
        but chances are
its no more stimulated than Achilles
dancing on dream shores of youth forevermore, way up
in an infinite sky   alive
                                        with galaxies
of fire   and   ice

where alleycats moan like demon babies
resting on the yawns of clowns, I got my share
of burdens, no nuisance
is gonna go away like the vagabond found a warmer train,

If the police don't get you, the IRS will
Plastic credit junkies sucking on the breast of war, wondering
How will we get more? More. More! M O R E ! ! !

Toking on the faraway moon it seems
hallucinations from afar illuminate
the rusting rain pipe, as morning drips
along
focusing
on the marvelous capacity
for invention

as compassion
 reeks
of grim observations of greed
necessity, we
weren't sent here for dimension,

       Sister, this ain't our season
       Come under the bridge, get out of the rain
       When you're poor they're gonna keep you down
     Don't get no delusions 'bout the noble intent of hounds
sweat some more and maybe
              M A Y B E
Someday there'll be some saint around
     showing intelligence and patience
to comfort your racked cerebellum hibernating fried by the
television,

    and leaving the unjust to stand before god.

A Buskin For The Frump

Lady Cynthia teaches school
  Arms the children with practical tools
  Gives them insight, help and hope
  When she goes home she's all alone,

Schoolteacher, I remember
Dressed with pretty young ambitions
  Justified such bold admissions
  Yet is left with no warm kittens,

    Schoolteacher, can I reach you?
  The coldness of your private life
  Has dulled the blade of your sharp knife
 You're old and gray what can be done
    To fill your long night hours with fun?

  Poor aging maiden, breasts once worth gold
void of such things that to others grow old
    Poor virgin widow on a timeless bold guess
That somewhere afar lies rewards for her best.

Industrial Disease

Everyday I come into this place in a good mood and leave like I
want to kill

I must like the job, or I hope I'm smart
enough that I wouldn't be here.

But fuck it. What satisfaction do I get?
A meager salary to live fat and irresponsible with?

People like me shouldn't have money.
People like me should have woods
To play in
tell stories in, and sing
                                        without offending anyone
To be alone in
and not be beaten down everyday
like every preoccupied face on the street
pounced upon, deflated
reduced to dwarfed televisiontelligence
shotgunned
  lobotomized

No longer looking for a sparkle in your eyes.

Opus 37

Winged birds in flight
Wind, life and ocean
Open your arms to me
Let me love you

Waves of destiny
Unknown and mysterious
Ominous and empty
I'm not the Earth

Who loves a cynic who isn't in love?
Not I said the spider, nor I said the bee.

Rapid water flowing downstream
                              Splashing
        Roaring
                        under the bridge beside the road
From the mouth of a monument
                                        to the sea
            whispers
      of life
  Inside a still rich forest
                              of evergreen ominous
            Native priests of the golden West
Who's as deep as a fool in love?
            Not I said the spider, nor I said the bee.

Painted doll
What color is your face?
What's all that in your weekend suitcase?
Call me a liar, call me a bum
I get my energy from the sun,

        trite romancer, Big screen lines
    don't you know what happens during fade out time?
      Let your hair get messed, your deodorant fail
            I wanna find you
        beneath your fashion veil,

I think
beyond logic
Answers Concrete
for a week I
Haven't slept with any wonders
haven't cared about the blunders
nor the neighbors, nor the price
The prize of life
is in your eyes
I am not whole
without your breath, your forest of light
shoulders, your voice
Spirit and sight
though I'm not what I might be
Ever could I be the lover of your dreams?
Don't deprive me please
of the ripeness in your eye tonight
Could I grow to hold you like tonight nobody could?
should I keep my dignity
or should I be
Love's fool again?

Life's essence on a tightrope
high above
the Casual fuckers
are they lovers too?
Is this experience something new
or is it

this game I keep playing and losing?

Are there no endless comedies?

a long road
Carrying a load
Superhighway swift and free
Overhead leaves
my aborted destiny

Fare ye well, fare ye well
now but my aftertaste sleeps with you.

Partially Made of Forest

gently flowing
she waves her hand across the treetops, full of birth

all as in a dream
the brightest grass beside the stream

hazy sunlight floods the meadow
awash with blood, commanding silence
nurturing

reaching, kicking

feeding

Searching for a breeze to keep the bugs away
proud walking, my
eyes maimed on inspiration, I

cross the stream washing clean each shore

and soothed, creep away

into her effervescent
splendor

Beat Blood
(For Allen Ginsberg)

Allen Ginsberg you must be an old man tonight
Friday some ancient geezer in the basement of City Lights
 who claimed to know you well who was probably mad told
Stories of you and Jack and Neil and he was one old ancient senile
fossilized grandad
And yet
I got your words of life in front of me now
and it seems to me you're young young young
And through all eternity you'll always be
Alive like old Walt brother teacher father
And me
I got my cosmos to tackle
America ain't changed much in twenty nine years
Folks still real damn serious about keeping the world insane
Tonight there's no rain, but somewhere a shoulder
        So who's growing older? None but the dead
Nineteen ninety two and still Nemo was right
It'd be nice to raise Blake from the depths
Gather a hundred hippies and go beneath the sea
With Lennon and McCartney in a yellow submarine as cool
As cocksman Cassidy's suitcase must've been
Where down below the surface we could ignore the strange
straight world
Boogie, create and be beautiful
And listen to what else Walt would say
Invite Shakespeare and Henry Miller
And Jesus if he promised not to preach
And Buddha, and Loa Tzu
  and all the other hipsters through the ages
But I wouldn't dare leave the world alone
To a handful of martyr type Martin Luther clones
To wrangle politicians and their flocks of wolf stalked sheep
When Earth is still a minefield of nuclear freaks
INSANITY   *INSANITY*   INSANITY
        What say you tonight old young man?
What'd you learn in those nut houses about man?
Before I lose my sense of humor, I want to understand
Why life and death can be perceived

as a bag of marbles rolling towards the gutter?
I don't really care because I love the clatter
and I see beauty in the ashes
Madness! Crazy as a burning match
I'm all through waiting for the reigns, I'm here
Born, signed, sealed, delivered just in time
To kick the ashes about and cough and laugh
And puke a little and lust a little
And search for God
    a little
And drool on the American dream
    a little
And hope to live long enough to elect a sane president
       for a change
While believing in a Superman
 who'll ride a missile just like Slim Pickens way out to the edge of
the universe
       far away
 So as not to destroy
our junkyard where
sunflowers still do grow
Eucalyptus, cacti
 rattlesnakes, grapes, streams
Grizzlies and their holy shit, HOLY S H I T !
Eliott spoke like an undertaker, Ain't no wasteland in me
I got beat blood inside me
Rich blood that points right to Cala Foods
I get a natural transfusion from this city of enlightened minds
A transfusion that grants sight and smell
  and sweet hallucinations
 and reality only in moderate doses
The blood that's come to me from you and Walt
A wild, pure river flowing
right through us, wanting to turn the world on
laughing as bones rot, because age is nonsense
I just want you to know that Allen, you queer honest poetic angel
Feeding your river
I'm gonna dump in my blood
It's eternity we leave behind
Tattooed on the brains of the misguided mortal.

Inside a Rainbow

Nobody questioned, cynically stagnating, trying to reach
the higher ground.

 oh brother, Strapped to the pack
the weight of another, take my twisted tongue back
try to get
a rebate check to pay
off what meager mortgage I have left
on my evaporating
soul,

Sometimes I grow so old
that darkness lasts forever
 and weary, even sunlight can't relieve
  the dreary deeds that foul up all bliss commitments,

Sometimes I grow so old
 that darkness lasts forever
creating anew, those ruins
        long since trodden passed,
Long since rinsed my aims of such ambitions
Yet Ego still takes the reigns and runs like folly over the plains
under the abstract, severing
near the shore
of common
chatter

in the supermarket line.

Surprise Encounter

Are we to remember that once we were lovers?
My heart beats intensely to look at you still, wedding ring and all,

While me and the dudes here are drowning in drink
I, standing alone, am shrinking
Trying to look pleasant while dancing with strangers
 who have nothing to say in the morn,
Dreaming suddenly of
your warm touch cooled from me now, while
so slow proceeds the promise of the peace I'm searching for
Killing time with kind hearts strung out on the floor
Well after midnight, these old songs are boring
I've faced the morn bit again and again
tried to drive these stinging tunes out
Again and again
cursed myself and my weakness again and again as
we move off to who knows where,

Now you're married
You, who said nothing's forever
Who I surrendered to
Who I feared so cause I couldn't ignore
You who I had dreams of old age with
Remember those promises? Recall the sincerity
And in between those lines we live
Growing cold or warmer from the wounds?

Incurable romantic, eyes shifting from tomorrow towards
yesterday
Driving on through unimagined dawns
Far from the city where above lust we shone
Projecting
innocence, we claimed unflinchingly wouldn't die
Yet,
 jamming blind into tonight, a strange respectability
somewhere beneath this fools disguise is trying to stay in tune
With music of the spheres, news and emotion,

Have I loved?
Have I given love at all?
What do I know of commitment? Creation?
What do I know of love?

I was a boy those short winters ago
Intrigued by all I couldn't have:
Golden prairie lands, magical marquees
Saving the planet, craving the simple
Dashboard lights and a highway leading forever,

With you it was a fresh new dance
I'm now, in this casual world of misfits, a man
And sparkling visions of eternity do appear
before me as I fear my spine a crumbling 'neath the weight
of insignificance, knowing
The ant and the deer have their function
As the rain and sea, but I
In sync only with the blasphemous trigger of society
Remain counter-productive, stagnating
with the mediocrity of cynical regression,

By the fire lighted reason of this universe tonight
I feel an echo of confusion interrupt the forest heights
Stumbling through revisions, lost dreams and hopes
Aloof inside these dancing flames
Swirling with gulls above cliffs beside the empire
Tending soft my garden mending
Toxins in the air, aware
That every breathing entity must have a care,

With you it was a first time dance
It's been years now since I've mastered romance
And through all the motions of near perfect scenes
Still inside I come apart at the seams, more often wondering
where went the magic
of the unknown, was innocence
the greatest flame
after all?

Valley of the Lightning Struck Forest

Born in a chicken hatchery and raised
on ABC and television praise
taught to walk tall, spend and rise
little did we know about
the potholes in the road

Me mE Me me ME, I got
no time on this Earth for you or who
ever made the fuse that lights the house and keeps the
heat and stereo on high
              , I got
too get in place
and groove
got
my own occupation, leisure, elevator comes soon

shit.
divine nation
under god,
catered materialists
universal misfits
 going the way of Rome

                    dried up, poisoned soil blows
                                        across highways and
horizons
                                    As racing to our sacred
destinations
                            endlessly sucking
                                    unquenchably
            from the Earth, we
 the hope and sorrow of tomorrow
blank, basted, kicking back
after narrowly panning for fools gold, let go the fad
irrelevant, creationless

maybe the ammo ain't so tame
but baby the jive is so ripe you can slice it
sharp without smudging, deep fruit delicious

maybe you got some old souls from the carnival
not too crazed, not too sane
not too bitter or not too straight
to jam on philosophy in the pouring rain
and crash the guarded gates of eden?

Rock'n roll your engines baby
I wanna know if love's gone lazy
bars, neon stars
satellite transmissions of electric guitars
we might as well be
on Mars

throwing china dishes at the wall.

One White Boat With One White Sail

One white boat with one white sail
Free sailing on a dark day's sea
Despite the stormy ocean raging
Madness, havoc to the land
This white boat sails peaceful
As if it needs no helping hand,

I touch the rampaged muddy shore
Which the sea has scarred with all its' scorn
I see the temper of the skies
Striking down their battle horn,

How then does this white boat sail?
How then does its' mast not fail?
Tossed among the towering waves
 Anger on the oceans face
How, so small, can it keep afloat?
How, so easily, sails this boat?

The white boat floats even farther out to sea
Far beyond what little sight I have in me

Sail on, small white boat
On through the everchanging sea
I wish you all that I can dream
To help you sail so easily.

An Acquaintance, Now and Then

On the day I moved into my house
I met the young punk lived next door
Defiant hair, dress and speech, he invited me to drink
whiskey while he cranked his heavy metal up
   (Same loud rebellion of my youth)
His pockets held
some LSD and other pharmaceutical delights well known
to elevate folks far
                              O   U   T
   of the somber reality of day

Rebelling, chugging, putting down
the government and this and that & the other thing
"Please partake," he wincing, offered "In this artificial stimulation.
The world sucks
too much to be straight,"
said he.

When suddenly,
so suddenly
So old and worldly did I feel
So calm, so sane, so sober, gaining
Insight and control; Guiding wisely, unconceited
Cautious that my desires were pure
I knew my only fear was death
and grew and grew all in one moment
Recalling loves that had long since passed
Places far away, faces alive in youth
Tales from times so wild they made my new friend smile
As I sat there on my weathered suitcase
In a room without a bed or chair
Answering gratefully at peace
"No thank you please,
I'm fine.

This moment is thick and there is no other
My head is heavy with intangible concepts soon to be at hand
I feel a tremor from a higher world
Sending sparks into this conscious world:
                                        Glimpses of golden
coherence

                                                    Lights to lead
the way
  towards an understanding that the immediate world is
    Complete
My blistered feet require no bandage
My unfurnished room needs not a chair
I am aware, present, impenetrable
An infinite universe growing from
    my heavy featureless head."

                              _j_î

Years later,
settled in my rocker chair
in a room with plants, art and affairs
when we'd begun to buy the farm together
dining on daily disasters, scurrying frenzied with indigestion,
still wondering about Amazing Grace
We
grew to speak from the same heart and tongue.

THE SYSTEM

1.

If the system you are using
is the system you are using
then the system you are using
must be the system that you use

if the system you are using
is the system you are used to
then the system you are used to
must be the system that you use

if the system you are used to
is the system that you need
then the system you are used to
must be the system for you

if the system you are used to
is a system that is harmful
then beware

for the system you are using
could be a system of despair.

2.

If want
to buck the system
don't make love to
the coffee machine,

if the system you
are inclined to bleed
from
is *you*
then *you*
might be what the system needs
if systematically speaking *you*

are what the system needs
then bleed some more,
humanity craves
a little more
phosphorescence
to adapt a creed

3.

I remember one night in san francisco
twas a night
inside a bar
the night before
I resumed school
the night after
I remember not

and what that's got
to do with diddly
I hardly know
and rarely care
and though I'm grow-
ing apathetic
please don't think
me unaware

I rest my collar
for the preacher
of another
age and time,
remember walking
truer streets
now smell the coffee
fresh as I find

Does this ballad
get you wondering
what lies beyond
your old routine?
Dreaming of cousins

long remembered
passed the twilight
of our teens,

Doesn't the defence
get you angry,
sheltered in your
suburban nest?

don't let the lack of
communication
be the downfall
of your breast.

and shall we whisper
anymore
in the dark against
the storm?

or shall we face
with unstrained passion
the neglect we've
grown to fear?

Hard decisions
life is short
special, precious
what shall we find?
what shall we leave behind?

4.

Oh, the blister
is not on your tomb
but a whisper
can relieve the wound,

and should you wonder
 do not worry
I shall be here

miserable
detesting
I shall be here

unable to divide my time between my love and life
adapting to the relevant and righteous
not two feet out of mediocrity
 I shall be here

Cursing the original curse and inspiration
Tossing it all up to rearrange for a show
All is progress
all is evolution
Damn the evolution   Damn the conformity!
Damn the damn damn the damn damn the damn damn damn
damn dam.

What does it take to
get it out of
your system when
the system you are using is
inescapable?

when the system you are using is
you?

when you get no rebate
no trade in allowance for
your soul?

and you can't afford
a new
one
(I'm a young
man, I don't
dream no
more).

5.

The system I am using
is a system non-efficient
a system for a scheme much larger than will reap a profit in
my lifetime

The system I am using is
a system I
can't quite make sense of
A system, I believe
containing the elements of
heart and soul
mind & toil
song and sweat
curse & dance
smile and tears
youth & years
wisdom and fear
the system I
am using is
a system from
the earth,
a system for
the earth
a system hum-
anity uses
to define
it's worth, a
system from
the eternities, a
system for
the universe:
chaotic, harmonic, yin/yang, left brain
right brain, drunk, sane
the system I
am using is
a system I
would like to share
not exclusively with
you but, everyone

at every time
all entities living and otherwise
we shall not rest
absent from
the rest

will you try
the system I
am using?

I have tried
the system you
are using.

6.

Can we smile
from pole to pole
and leave each other
free to roam?
or must we make
a creed and keep
ourselves together
or apart?

must we start anew
or die together?

can we all
be born anew
in each others hearts?

7.

Gagging on soccer
Aging on overtime
Dragged out by last year
Looking for this year

Hanging out searching
where went the days?
Now comes the taxman
and empty praise

Knocked on down
by bowling hall bruisers
daisies on airplanes
What does it mean
to have dreams of scary people huddling in the mud-soaked
wonder?
nestling in imposed routine?
bidding adieu to once grand dreams
scorning the child who hasn't let go
drawing up ammo for common sense logic
havoc on a commuter train, isn't it so
far from the warm brow smiles embracing?
Far from acoustic guitar by the fire
out in the forest, harmonizing with trees
crickets and breezes, dancing, singing as they brush
against each other,

I've had enough

of city ways beat into crazed workdays
trying to keep up with the economic race
trying to keep greed from the door
while visitors come crying

"More! more! more!"

I would like to trade my system in
I would rather feel your heart again
I would like to rub our toes together on a fresh field of grass
and would like the world to emulate your tenderness

Yet the snows keep falling black, tarnished by industrialized
sweat
The sow is empty, the vat is cheapened
as we struggle more and more to raise our heavy flag and hope
the wind
 will keep it flying once again.

Another War

Our mirrors reflecting heaven, shatter
turning the plane beyond to hell
Oilfield infernos burn black the sky, smothering waters

a fever breaks, squinting
from the light of youth's grand promise
in common duds unfavorable
hoisted from the army dumpster of salvation

and if I were triumphant
would I curse again the aim
or wander forth through twisted notions of my own utopia
slumbering in the ease of moral luxury
above the needy servants of the tomb?

¥

A Pint Of Guinness

A pint of Guiness for me mates
  A half pint for myself,
It's not that I'm a lightweight
  but me name don't ring with wealth;

To me mates who've never failed me
  I pledge my life and brau,
The date wouldn't be appealing
  If not for your good shouts;

Pour them each that precious stout
  I've no selfish need, not now
For in the company of me mates
  I'll drink just up the hour.

Crazy Lady Poet

Pink leotards and a short black skirt, she smokes
  her cigarette and flirts
Tossing free her long brown hair
Turning her suitors into grizzly bears who take
  her magnetic bait and are snagged
As she winks her long eyelashes and grins
  Digs in her purse and pulls out a book
  of poems she's written and will now rehearse,

Don't let her scare you because she's got
A gum chewing grin and a know-it all eye
So superior are the moves she contrives
But all the way through she's alive

She cries and she whispers, she's so cool and tame
Sometimes she'll even confess without shame, She
  screams, shed's tears and blushes sincere

And yet
  In the bar corner she looks so severe.

That crazy Lady Poet
Once kicked me in my head at dawn
  To wake me up with crazy lines
Of love and thirst
  Bursting art and tied emotion
Breakfast made of vowels
  Verbs and mesmerizing tones
  Lady, you've outgrown your bones
Releasing reigns of ridicule
  "I love you and you and you" she says
  "and every seedy character
  Suspicious, full of mischief"
I knew it all soon after dawn
  She never hid a single thought
  "Achieving is a lot like teasing
  "Emotions are what's really pleasing"

I climbed into her wild machine
   Through stoplights honking horny
        On a holy Sunday morning when
 She sold a stack of books for bread and butter
  bouncing a check to the theater
While testing her thoughts on strangers
   Who barked back clueless, staring
That crazy lady poetess for her words is proudly starving

Crazy Lady's workshop is
 A run down flat with shredded doors
        That crazy Lady Poet had me laughing on the floor
            Reading aloud while cooking slop
                Horrid stuff i couldn't swallow
                Yet she served it proud
Strumming crummy chords and singing sour
Until the audience all went deaf
And left.

            Crazy cosmopolite of emotion's abstract waves
Madonna of heaven, on Earth's shores we roam
        Where nothing is perfect, nor sweet as your song
Where?
Where is this hour? Where is this place?
    What city? What century? What season? Your face
                Sets off those nerves that explode self
control
As inside you glares something that's hard to resist
Is it mystery? Is it magic?   Romance?   Or your kiss?

                                        Crazy

calm collector
                    Of simple minded truths
Serene contemplator
        Of a life so far removed
Loudly shouting lullabies
                    To relive the wounds of enterprise
While your lines intertwine
    With the sadness in your eyes;

Crazy Lady Poet, Love longs to lay with you
But you instead bestow it
To words that faint around you,
Crazy Lady Poet
Promise me a sonnet
I admit to knowing
Nothing of your lingering breath
Yet my heart beats on your breast
Am I a shadow like the rest
On your wall of emptiness?
Here rotting away on the inside
As you're there looking away towards the door,
Tell me, oh tell me, what symbol is this?

Crazy Lady Poet please
Come tug at me some more
It's your confidence in wisdom
That scrapes me off the floor
Me a careless, reckless bum
Beside you new sensations come
Inside you lies work never done
Always on the run crazy lady
What do you do for fun pretty baby?
What can I do to make you stop
And listen to yourself for once?

Lady take my hand again
It's evening and I need a friend
Such tenderness is mockable
But toughness isn't possible
In moments like these measured out
by silent, soft submissions

Lay your wild thoughts down, sweet lady
Lets make life from your poetic vision.

And all night long she held me
loving 'til the break of dawn
as sensations fine were won
In the flesh not on a page
That weren't devoured by the day

The Net

There's no way to stop
dangling on the ol' farm fence
when you been up high
at the mighty height of serious intoxication
There's no way
to keep your habits
from getting hellbent, no way
to distinguish
the apple from the rye
no way
to keep the hustlers off your mind, not when
there's been a rumor spread
that heaven's been
a lie,

Ain't no way to jam out rock'n roll when ancient is your waning
soul
and any grip upon the quaking ground is just a cobwebbed vision
after all
and far away are all the groupies you dream about that play your
game
when
the fact is
there's
no
umbrella for the existential rain.

And your reign upon the earth just dwindles
soon you've none to pass
as the scoundrels come a begging for the last shirt on your back
then it takes a smidge of character to reconnect
with whatever it is that keeps one
free in the sea
swimming, avoiding
the net.

Candice

Candice, the afternoon at hand
'll be bland if branded by a clocks swift hand
Let's rebuke the days routine
and see if we can intervene

Please, the baker's calling me
and I don't really want to be
Baking on this sunny day
Sweating by the oven's flame
Let's sneak out and see if we
can catch a glimpse of eternity

Candice, there's many things to do
Now time is on our side, let's
abide by youth's velocity and be bright sails on the wind
We won't be rocking
the world cause
there are no original sins
At worst we'll put our past to shame, at
best we'll murder our routine, Today's worn scheme
is all so petty, are you ready
to run out and swim?
Just us two and solitude
Swelling to new magnitudes
We won't be starving poor today
Penniless, our hunger makes us
Bland we'll never be Candice
While richness rules the atmosphere
Now Time is on our side, are you ready
to run out and swim
amidst the true
brief
passing tides
of life
?

Letter to a Bush

Mr. President,

Scared of this world?
I been hearing quite a lot of ugly
truths

Sorry truths

Painful reminders that life just ain't bliss
Unquenchable hipsters can't stand being miffed
Unprecedented bogusness, bonanza gone wrong
Man,
I can't even look, the view
is so fucking smoggy ain't no
Absolutely No!
Concern
, care or comprehension of eternity at
ALL,
      MAN
DON'T KNOW ABOUT YOU BUT MY BROTHER'S COOL
MORE THAN i GOT MY SHIT TOGETHER
MORE THAN i CAN CONTROL MY AGGRESSION AND
WHAT'S YOUR PROBLEM
WITH MY RESISTANCE
TO YOUR TRUTH?
WHAT'S WRONG
WITH MY ATTITUDE?
Man, I'm worried 'bout yours
You on the pedestal, I on the mudpie
You so condescending when I don't understand
What kind of Man
are you?
Your world is filled with death
Your world isn't redempt
Your veneer clear is gloss but underneath your frost kills

and you're so cut off
so racing in circles, treadmills
malls of america
man,
I'm not gonna fight in your Goddamned war
kill and slay for the sake of blood-soaked oil
for our national greed nor our shameless debt
nor pride or salvation, when it says in your Bible
THOU SHALL NOT
KILL.
PERIOD.
Not Amend Section A, Except when national pride or economic
well being is at stake or when our leaders start blaming someone
for being Satanic when the evidence CLEARLY
shows our own sins
to be no less
(greater, actually)
                                        What bullshit. Let it all

  wilt away
                I'm tired
of playing irrelevant games   keeping
the economy
greedy and fat so
someone somewhere gets lean and ratty raping
   brother
 Earth sister
  Soon moon and as far
    as we can go, to
keep up to those out of touch Tom Hanson's since birth, seems
to keep grasping for more, well
                          F U C K   T H A T !
I want to caress this sweet body beside me
wanna feel the cool earth and warm sea, but it seems there

              ain't no way to make that consumer sting go away.

                          Born with that need
to consume, as desire
    out of tune tripping on high voltage wires carrying infant fed
grand untrue dreams,
relates

more illusions
        and out of state plates, seems
ain't no way
to rap with the facts with a full honest hand
seems you gotta have a scam to walk tall with the man

It occurs to me, Mr. President
that a proud and moral nation would not spend a whole lot more
money on bombing the shit out of another country than it spends
on eliminating the deficiencies of its own country.

And it occurs to me
that a proud and moral nation would not hate
Such as I hate you now.

appalled by quick acceptance of preposterous lies put forth, I'm
horrified
by Hitler's Germany out
to create a new world order,
Crushed by ignorance and apathy
I feel part of no proud moral nation

Mister President please
let all your bullshit wilt away, please
Discourage your fervor of trite right and wrong
redeem unwanted storms by ravishing your manifold
Let us people be
people.

Let our cultures
have our heritage
let us dream and dance, enrich
let our human hearts be haunted
by poetics of internal wandering, peaceful to the world at large
Kindly drain, if you will, you're obsolete manifestos in a bottle
Mr. President,
and throw that fucker far
out to the end of the black cosmic sea
of eternity
                        and lets clear the air of all this obstruction
and see if we can recognize waning species flying boldly

to tomorrow through
the graying air.

Sincerely,

Monday morning hung

Stray Dogs

Late night hoping for a little private love
          intimate and life renewing
When out of the alley comes a yelp and a hobble
Another lost cause, it's a familiar routine
A stray dog comes to check out the scene,

Have I become so elitist? So cut-off, so cruel?
As to denounce all the fools and think like machines
of perfection? Independence? Of grand yuppie scenes
 so as there is no room to share
         or care for the lost?

She would rather fall prey to accident
Than leave a lone pup aloof
Diving through dumpsters of abandoned riches
Where she, beneath the falseness, dwells
Queen of streetwise misfits
Chef to untrained pallets, knowing
  only hunger and hope,
and the choke of the hanging rope,

Late night hoping for a little private love
After slaving like a moron in the profiteering mold
Not for redemption, art, humanity or boldness only
To keep the wolves away
from the door she opens graciously,

And there we stay exhausted
Overcrowded and divided
Questioning the karma and the aim of all the bulls
Vigilantly surviving on the cocky curse of fools
Knowing that in heaven
  There'd be no such regulation
As reigns to run the daylight hours so rampant
 Neglecting human sores
  so prevalent and fated,

Late night hoping for a little private love
Intimate and life renewing, as she sneaks
        out the back door to feed
Vagabonds like me.

Jazz

Booze all over the floor
The place is destroyed
And the crowd wants more
Verses
        Of a hopeful reality,

There she was
Against a white wall, a silhouette talking
About the depth of human beings
Her dreams

While her tough guy lay wounded on the sofa
Knocked out by drink

And waiting for silk to please
His mistress and need
Her poor man sulked on the floor

Where a misguided bore
Romanticized his visions

While the strange black cat purred
And we listened.

A Myth Called Freedom

I spent a little time on the mountain
I spent a little time in Zanzibar
But most of my time is spent
in Babylon
trying to communicate with
those
who remind me of
myself.

It's perfect formulation
It's abstract manifesto
It's all that's necessary to keep the brain liquid and flowing
Dreaming temporarily of goddesses unloved
who ought to be
who I should be with now
Instead of dreaming into machine
instead of scheming on tomorrow
willing, they
are salvation

Yet, who is one when love is all?
And why is fate when faith has stalled?

thinking about
it all, thinking about
Hamburger Haven, back when
life was simpler and
poetry was everything and
those few I knew where all that mattered

reflecting now
the problem is
that I'm too stoned
and too many is
restriction

and I don't want to groove on pygmies when they don't all want
to groove on each other

dividing my heart up like the Earth
a war has so many wounds
and my brain like a ping pong ball, frustrated bounces
irrelevant
between lost causes

as I
like the sap from a spring maple
dreams tapped delinquent
a shooting or shot star from a galaxy apart

drop sweetly down the weathered bark,

and if only it weren't criminal to try and change
notions of heaven,
I wouldn't be so poor today, I wouldn't be
a slave like all those thinking they possess freedom when

it's just a bubble
to babble about.

_*%_

Busy Mary, Freelance Fred

Busy Mary, Freelance Fred
Made Ed in a beat up Ford or Chev
Mary's Ma cried, her old man got his gun
And Freelance Fred, he hit the road,

Blurry motivations lead Mary to confession
On a jukebox saturday night rocking mindless
Hanging out waiting for a cosmic occurrence
As tears in her swinging tight jeans were lost,

The killer on his holiday rides in the rain
Holding his head up, dreaming of love
Seeing stars and vultures through stoned cool eyes
He tips his hat to the prettiest wives.

Wartime

I got my badges
out of the dresser and marched militantly sad down the street
Along with other weeping grievers who
of late had so much faith
that humanity and perhaps even our government
was getting a little hipper,

But I should have known
We all should have known
But what with all this talk of peace breaking out
Berlin Wall coming down, Gorby coming to town
Wellstone winning the Senate to Washington...
It was a short brief light of inspiration
Once again shot down
to
the reality that
Our world is built on war and War
Alone
Will dominate
our world.

And so we shift beliefs to keep
our sanity knowing never
will the meek inherit

Now we know and proudly toast
this is the best war, the proudest, the most
just and moral step we have taken
We, as a Nation
 a self righteous collective identity
flattered by the smell of victory within;

Drinking down the last call after closing time
trying not to sober, trying not to care
trying not to pry into unfathomable events
one can't do anything about

Cause they've rehearsed it all
Grenada, Panama, dress rehearsals for
The FREEDOM bowl
The kickoff all takes place at prime time
The anchormen are there
So we
can drink and hear the bombs fall
And watch the anchors scramble
to put their gasmasks on in terror
As Scuds streak across Israeli skies
we'll watch the madness and the stock market rise,

And that's the way it'll be
The schools'll have to hold another bake sale
To hell with the tree hugging freaks and the homeless
When it looks like we're crawling we'll get up and pounce
cause there's no stopping a nation
under god
that makes its best tools for war.

For the Next Free Key Child Comin' Along

Ain't got a date and the moon's sinkin' low
ain't got much hatred, yet only one dose
of love
I've been saving for
 the next
freaky child
     comin' along,

                    Why is love? and is it such an easy treat?
                              When the soul tears, burns, rips, scattering
                                        out to the rain soaked road, thumb
out wondering
                    Where is the land of our heaven dreams?

it could be
it could not be,
it really doesn't matter
to me

I could be alone tonight
as well as with you
I don't know
 what
 I'm fearing,
doing?
               Where do we begin?
end?   in the grand

          cosmology of it all,

Ain't got a date, now the moon's sinking lower
Can't fake a smile when the scent of love turns sour
Still ain't got much hatred
   somehow saved that special dose
of love
   I was saving for
you.

The Man Who Watches The World Stumble

Perhaps it's all but travesty
What two eyes will see and know
What one heart will feel, one brain discover,

One tongue can't speak perfection
One language cannot say it all;

In what shallow sorrows lie
  more potency than promise?
As deep beneath a fools disquise
  Lies what besides a person lost?

The man who watches the world crumble
Can only stumble himself to find
The treasure lies beyond the time
He's spent mocking the rubble.

Castles In The Sand

Castles in the sand
Isn't everything we do but castles in the sand?

Value the laughter ringing through the trees
These are those things which I'll never let go
Imagine a forest where life doesn't whisper
These hours would pass away without triumph,

I ponder and wander and come to no end
Carrying proud foolish weight for a time,
To add some gems to our bland halls of ruin
Reaching beyond our graffiti stained walls
Good graffiti, bad graffiti
All us leave our mark as each
fall is saved by arms embracing,
Big, bony, loud, petite -- all are the flowers,
As too often blind, we fight to stand
Building castles in the sand.

Oh Baby

Vindicated, syndicated and shaved away
Oh baby,
let me ease your shivering, it's
all
that really I'm qualified to do,

and if you think
       wonder
for my love may be a blunder

does that make it any less thrown off the path?

and if you drink
with me from my soiled cup
I shall try not to offend you
by blaming you for the tarnished mug.

Eternal Meditation

A single flower
thwarted by thistles
alone amidst a hostile desert

Love, what of
love? I wonder of perfection
Wander dreaming to return
To her who holds me, blossoming, as I consider
Past encounters, weighing
each pro and con, it's hard
to measure

Have I grown slow
Or is this pleasure?

Love, what of love?
Such eloquence in wondering
'bout deeds delivered true as rolling tumbleweed across a canyon
vast.

Is this flower so sacred?
So perfect? Brilliant? Alien?

The commanding wind
 Like a hurricane rips
Petals off the unprotected
 Scattering the barren land with color
Perhaps to seed, perhaps
To rot with carcasses of
 another truth,

Of love, I wonder, touched
By simple deeds, can't judge
By sweeping vows of devotion
        Can't live up to the myths

No free and easy sail on everchanging winds
No eternal intoxication nor sweet enduring blossom
Dangerous
 as thorns snag the heart
ripping open a wound, deep, exposed
 as time unravels
mysteriously serenading the unconscious,

Love's beauty is all in another dimension
Invisible
to the naked eye, elusive
 yet surrounding, inescapable
Like shadows in the setting sun
deepening
to make a bed, a
triumph of warmth
Against the turbulence of
Our hellacious world of paradise.

Long Terms

You
love
and
change

round me hurting hanging upside silly down prone to love
songs,

it surely seems
like smell the dew
only lying back in a dream,

 yet making love still sings and brings
vibrations near true as ne'r the cynic thought could be.

As Babylon Lays Dying,
a brand new child wakes smiling

Coming in and coming out
trying to shout out loud and grin
trying to cool a fire within
so I know that I've been born
into this world filled with scorn,

Stoned to the floor, gasping
whispering once again
wondering where I am

who i am

On the floor
I adore
Whatever light might to shine in
alive again dumbfounded

with a grin
Regained the glory lost
by chasing wrought, Where have I been?
What light have I been
chasing?
and what goal could I have possibly adored
more than living?
Have I been a bore?
Longing for tomorrow's sun
I love breathing, only being, bleeding
seeing all the rest
Loving the seasons
snow above the rest
Laughing at the reason
of such trite happiness
Singing out the door
blind by knowledge
hid away by emptiness demanded
vanished in thin air, pursuing
drifting like a cloud
up in a worshipped sky,

What is it
    we're after?
        Would a kiss
            outweigh this laughter?

       It really makes no sense
       but everyone climbs fences
     and sailboats go stoking up the sun
      while losers sail in search of fun
              strapped
         by a longing to communicate
Shadows
moving on the wall
(it's not I that's tall)

      Trapped within
      lost without
   Shouting agony
     seeking harmony
      Buying prescriptions at the pharmacy
    relieving the drudgery with drink
    Lose the stance
  romance flies off
    found solitude
    in a dusty loft
               Aloof
      from foreign and familiar
A spoof

to those who looked up laughing.

     Seagulls flying in midair
     Cold winter morning stares
    out the window if we dare
    The wind blows it's own wear,
Another day lies down
   I wave so long and frown
     it's light didn't shine eternally
      and all its deeds will fall,

One day fades away
then two, then six
Where then do we pick up the sticks?
Backed into a corner
lost the change, lost the age
Lost all muttering moments away
Comfortable, Cantankerous
wondering about the space untravelled
mysterious faces not yet unravelled
temptations in the playpen while
outside the season's changing
Life is always rearranging.

Kiss me long so I
know a base
It's lonely lost
alone in space
Travelling at an unsure pace
Frightened of
disappearing,

On the Earth
in it's realm
Time and dimension
cast a spell
time flies
Faces change
lifestyles
Rearrange
Thoughts so new, they come and go
everything by itself does grow

Baking the bread yet fresh for the week
Baking the bread for the weak to eat
Baking the bread for the thrill and joy
A taste of the bread serves to grow the boy.

* * * * *

Waking
Really waking
Not into a dream
Into a loud world of complete
serendipity

Travelling through time and space
It's quite a place that I wake up in
a lonely traveller tempted by pleasure
ain't got a penny for my thoughts
but I love this day I've got
full of sun, wonderful sun

Clear, frosted winter's day
With pride I comb my hair and wash
my weatherbeaten skin and watch
the feelings in reaction to each noble thought
and weakened, then set forth in sorrow
to lift sincerity with laughter
and after all the drink is gone
I hang and contemplate each wrong
And hear an echo from a temple
Sometimes I wish that I was there
Instead of lost in chaos found from
a mind open wide,

Inside do I tremble when
mortality is ringing, infinity is singing
a melody comes knocking on my door
nothing more,

sadness carries out
a hundred useless doubts
Bugs come crawling up my spine
while rowing through the waves of day
Eternity, still far away
and carrying on but without song
Clouds seem awful stron
Here I contemplate that sorrow
Trembling
while my stomach spews

Fine in flesh, Pains of soul
so very young and far from old
Dreams of childhood sold
to schemes that somehow drain the hours
Spending time, Racing reckless
finer feelings oft are felt
and sweltering towards death shine weighted
while dated, all the monuments
are raked over for new importance
Hence do blossoms bleed
To make way for blessed new seed.

Think of life without a melody
Rhythm would rot away
Today will fade, tomorrow too
for just a moment I'm in tune
No thoughts of burden, no emotion wild
Nothing much to say but how I dread this moment leaving,
Nothing much new sensed except
a slice of peace
amidst the fading
afternoon,

I hear an echo from the temple
feel the thunder of the skies
and I know it's just a mirror
A reflection of my cries, I lay
my male body down to sleep in lullabies
that will not keep me
smiling until night again
and so I wake
to walk again.

It always leaves me unfulfilled
these big production numbers,
while the simple stirs in life
unexpected, seem to reign.

I'll trade the month
for just a moment
marked by ecstacy
don't care for coins
or greed, or things I need
no, just a love to seed

as Earth spins
and seasons change
as faces age while places fade to pages of the past
Today, at last
is all that's left

A theft of time has stolen
Prime personas, my madonna
So now I must to face today
Lace up my boots and walk
among what's risen.

Roots in the soil and mind with the wind
My old wet boots walk timid.

Ah devotion soothe the flame
Like an ocean, none's so tame.

It's not a good word, nor was I
When I spit up my frustrations at another
mattering less, it matters not

so many words are spoken
What is said?
As many verses written
What is read?

What secrets shared in bed
are remembered in the morn?
What surprises singed by ridicule
Live to deviate the norm ?

                                        I sink beneath
                                        The words I say
                        there is no greater glory today

            This sea of wisdom has no rock

                    I jump for joy
                    with no restraint
                            by evening joy
    Will just be faint

                                                all the miles in the
    day
                            Unending, not repeating

And now,
When it seems all words are said and done
The hours that are left
Carry more weight than those old logs burned,

To find peace and then to keep it
 is such a precious comedy,
A brief chill chasing faint up my spine;

as sky rockets commemorate
the fading away,

That deathly wind
drifts over the road
and over
Dreams of Grecian summer sun
dreams never fully realized.

Realizing this I hiss
Then I kiss the monolith

Tuning senses to appreciation
Collecting energy from the flow,
The apple is sweet
Taste it with me
and the rich scene I see
Can you see it too?

that glow on the horizon
is nothing more than a faint glimpse of truth,

A sharp eye sees no star is bland
Propaganda's not truth and sweethearts tell lies
In earnest we rise from the poison
In harvest, the purest are only the true;

 Wake now
but hold forever
that which to you is sacred,

The rhythm of the night train
carries me to where

I walk soft

dancing on a cold hard street called nowhere

Jazzman let your purpose echo

Never go away

Enhance this unrealized day

Let

Our inner cosmos echo through the outer spaces

Let us leave, at least
Our souls
Joyfully, painfully, but honestly exposing
that we have lived.

GrUngE

Dead Old Poets

Speak a dead old language

Words of ancient trivia

Don't care much about their face

Not those dead old poets who've

survived oblivion to

become cursed and second guessed, dissected

Who cares of their dead old pains? Who

Mourns still for those dead old poets

Who probably were half insane?

m   e

                        a   n   d
    w   h   a   t   a   b   o   u   t
    m   e   ,   s   h   a   l   l   I   b   e   f   I   l   l   e   d   ?
                            i know not
                            fullness
                          of life, being
                            care not
                      for redemption, only want
            to breathe the fresh full dawn today and come
            cleansed of soul destruction, i wanna feel
          feeling that outweights destructive yesterdays
                    Let all that bullshit wilt away
                        i wanna fall in love
                      with just one woman and
                      i hope that woman will be
                            you
                                                            .

Ghosts

Ghosts in the morning, ghosts in the noon
Ghosts in the mirror staring back at you
Ghosts in your bedroom tea, ghosts in your bath
Ghosts in the rickety rackety pick-up toolshed

Ghosts are sublime, anytime
There are ghosts uncertain, in gladuous handbags
Ghosts in disposable, dismal dispositions
Ghosts, as a matter of fact
Ghosts, *ghosts...*

Fiction or remote crawldaddies?
Picture this, a laughter shy
of insurmountable intent --
Visions are a blight, hellbent
on sunny everafters flickering
in earth-toned armaments and
wicker rockers by the flames
that warm the hearth.
Ghosts!

Ghosts in a wild, gnarley beard
Ghosts in a cobwebbed attic alibi
Ghosts in the cosmic warp of creation
Ghosts are the intrigue of the nation
Ghosts!

Ghosts of lost civilizations
Come setting up cantina mirages in the midnight fog
Decieve and repeal the landscape indescrimantly
Breathe and moan eirrie chants between vast canyon walls
Ghosts,
Ghosts, Ghosts

Ghosts reveal the bread and butter thrust
upon stagnant air and crumbled,
Ghosts cause fatigue, ghosts cause pain
Ghosts can drive mortals insane
Ghosts are uncanny, ghosts are cruel
Ghost'll drown friends in the swimming pool
Ghost's can redeem, ghosts can refrain
Ghosts'll make mountains out of the rain

Ghost'll swell panic, kill adventure and reign
Over the cobwebs up in the attic
Extinguishing the freshness of dew
Embellishing much deeper hues
Administering junky blues and delusions
Devisions
Ghosts are the seasons
Ghosts are the earth
Ghosts voice their fury up in a burst
Ghosts blow amo, ghosts fill their cups
And drink to the vacancy in all of us.

Aged Baby

Savvy leather
Meager leecher
magenta mean
your touchdown scheme
is coming out
of the sky
sliding on
the ice, falling
on whimsy, kissing peace
to le' machine
as techno cream
makes ergo easy
sneezes breezes
flapjack pantry
animated, ner sedated
backwards facts
straightforward shot
commodore caught
pants down prancing
through the fancy
unreality
of conventionality, licking
dry the prize grown
from smooth, white flesh thrown
boning sun, moving
on grooving
dawn's shadows
as
earthly immortals dance
divine
upon the swallowed chalice
of dismayed fate.

Lovingly

Loving
Loving
Tenderly
Loving,
Longingly
Passionate
Steamy hot
Love suds
Flowing
Juices, rivers
Touching
barren banks, wishing
practical death downstream
intoxicating
enhancing
animating
saving

tearing
aching,

Where do we Go from Here?

Piss poor beat up downtrodden
hanging lingering taxing
waning on a waiting elevator
gravity drawn to the core
begging the anecdote for more

out of the junkyard and into a garden
No enlightenment hanging in suicide alley
Every soul seems to care for the progress of destruction
sober, unsatiable
alien

ragged, worn and dated
say a prayer
to the heavens, to earth
recall the season of your birth
unaborted, a success
lived to walk these crucial steps
petrified
on ascension.

bullshit

fucking
goddammit

gonna
hungover
lennon
sase

shit

asshole!

authored
badass
bitching
bonkers
birkenstock
bullshit
c'mon
cappuccino burbs
chrissakes
clankety
clickety
cluelessly
crackerbox
dammit
darren
doubletalk
em-
barcadero
flowerchild
floyd
flusher
fucked
up
fucking
g a n j a !
godawful
gilligan

goddammit
gonna
goosebump
getta
hel-
lacious
hendrix
hangover
juke
looney
loverless
meanie
nuked
onlooking
pee
pissed
poetics
proposed
raggedy
restroom
rock'n
sandles
sartre'n
shit'n
smartass
skinhead
unaroused
undestined
imagined
wannabee
warm
whatdo
y'know
?

the drug of love

how bewildering it can be,

I don't know
if I am a free man or if cats from unconcious psychedelic
apprehension are flashing or if its just fatigue

this drug

of love

Day by Day

Sometimes day ain't worth a dime
Oft times dimes ain't worth a damn
The wonder of life multiplies to a haze
That gaze of youth gone grows to pain
Knowing the paths motivating our kind
Blowing out ego steam to rise above crimes
Ecologic degradation, intellectual despair
I been there,

Sometimes I try and find my out
Running free of responsibility
Others times boulders are far too much
To weigh upon my meager seed

Sailing the breeze
Sometimes,

ain't no way to make the pain go away

Sometimes

the tunnel to the rainbow is but a television dream
and life has no greater cohesion it seems
as bellowing like killing smoke
the righteous lose their good effect
and defects all, we curse the net
that plucked us out of the great free sea
of eternity

as we die together
cursing our collective fate

while the big fisherman drops his cigarette butt
on the bottom of the boat, it sizzles

in the water.

stone poem

```
        g               o               t
s               o               u       l               ?
```

L otta ev ol u tion
's gonna come yer way,
better start waggin'
yer tail and high
tail it towards that insurmountable summit
of yer frantic and relentless dreams

Footbridges to art sailing backwards, belly flop,

A   I   n   '   t   i   t

S u b u r b a n   n i g h t m a re, a i n 't it

Bob dylan, ain't it

Neil Young

and flannel shirts

and holy pits of eternal despair, kiss my

thanks for the salvation,

ain't it bob

dylan ain't it mojo

nixon ain't it hendrix

taken back facts ain't it

cobwebbed confusion ain't it

scent of love it ain't

reason, ain't

no easy

season, ain't

big picnic

trite beatnik

spent noodnick

at night frightning

lightning shattering

hidden prairie clothed

in black mystery, ain't

hid in a closet, part

of this world now, feel

the fife and drum

ripe and hum-

ming engine of humanity, oiling

sockets and joints

spoiling rockets and innuendoes

boiling ferver in soothing spiced herbs foiling the

manufacturer of doom, if there is

such a demon

such demeaner

has no consequence upon

the relator of fate

      acknowledging

      true fear awaiting

      belated

      love poems unsacred.

PASSION

I JUST THOUGHT THAT WORD MIGHT LOOK NICE
HANGING AROUND RIGHTERS AND TOO HIP MUSICIANS,
ACTORS, SPIES, CYNICS, VISIONARIES
CORONARIES, COBWEBS, CUD CRITTERS
-- ALL CRUISIN'
TO THE MORTUARY TOOLSHED ON A WHEELED TABLE
WHIZZING DOWN THE WHITE HALL, WIND BLOWIN''
MERRY
HAPPY AS HAMSTERS BREAKING OUT OF THE HABIT-TRAIL
NO BRADY BUNCH PORK CHOP'S"N APPLE SAUCE FOR
DINNER
ONLY SLIMMER
FATTER PRICED BLOTTER BUST CHOKE AND PUKE MUCK
SERVED FAST
SWALLOWED FASTER RACING RAT RACE, SPENDING,
DYING, HAMMING UP
ANY UNNECESSARY TIME UNKEPT

PASSION

TO BE BORN AGAIN

TO BE *SAVED*

TO NOT BE DROWNED A SLAVE

TO BE REMEMBERED

DELIVERED

TO HEAVEN'S GATE, *PASSION*

TO BE ABSURD

CONCRETELY

DISCRETELY

WONDERING OF FANATICS BLISTERED AND BITTEN

BY INTERNAL WARS AGGRAVATED BY DEALINGS WITH

LITTLE REALITIES,

WONDERING

S T I L L

IF WE'RE ALL CONNECTED IN SOME WAY OR

IF WE'RE JUST BABBLING ON IN OUR OWN MONOLOGUES

PICKING UP BITS

AND PIECES FOR FUEL VIA THE TELEVISON SCREAM,

STEREO CRANKED,

SPANKED, TANKED AND   TAINTED WITH CAKED ON SOAP

SUDS WHILE

FRYING IN THE OZONE FREE SUN WAITING

FOR SOMEONE

TO STOP ALL THIS

SUFFERING.

God,

bless this night of drinking

May we wake up in the morn

may the frolic mock the storm

and the aftermath be infamous

Blooms a night ridiculous

As me and all me mates of folly

lighten our heads and howl jolly

Singing to the silent sky

Staggering free down unknown streets

Yes'n

bless our blinded way oh Lord

so that we don't crash our Fords

and may morning bloom in brilliance as well

So as never do we curse our fate

Amen.

INITIAL DEPARTURE

Visual stimulus before the trip
                           Time and space manipulation
    finger on the thermostat
          poetic turbulences w i r l   n g
                              Outside   a   i   r
          Ever the window
Lights down   Heat up

          R)e(a)d(y f!o?r.   e|x|p|e|r|i|e|n|c|e

          Wierd music lights up the sky with lightning
     Completely whole no fraction
                              Why is the real world?
                    What is it made of?
          Where begin and end?
What for?

                    Skip the head-
                                   lines
                    Read the small
                                        print
Between

     lines without a tint,

               If not love tis needed happiness

                              This purely animal

          affair

bags packed, waiting to unwrap

the soul

Before walking the devouring some more

The dark cold endless stroll

don't make

plans alone

It's not healthy for the soul

Time's a petty measurement

The daily news hasn't heart

Shadows cast by

venetian blinds

Love is

warmth in those shadows

Catch the nearest sun

Inevitably the long night comes .

Girl in a Movie

Thinkin' 'bout a girl in a movie

Don't know none look like that, not Around here

Thinkin' 'bout that girl in the movie, Thinkin'

'bout time wasted on the assembly line

and the old lady wasting away,

Thinkin' 'bout love getting wasted, thinkin'

'bout it all the time instead of driving

Love home

Thinkin' 'bout that girl in a movie, thinkin'

'bout how I could live there with her

And thinkin' 'bout the old lady wasting away

While I'm thinkin' 'bout a girl in a movie,

Thinkin' its time to love and let go

of images found in a movie..

Heavy Irish Bailey's Brew

Neon Blackbird, disaster covered creampuffs
Hot hallucinations ugly gutterbrained masterminds
Upper ovens baking, sentimental works of art
Cold turkey ducks loafers hot seaweed platter void
of all complacent dreams which
freeze Reaching beyond eons of emotion scraping rust
We rise above dust
Down through valleys dark with decision
Where meddling madmen reroute noble dreams
Sunken seas beyond the storm
Open ends to tie and conform
Perform thou raggedy wrangler of life!
Some bonded in strife to the end of awakening
Set free those tigers to be timid no more!
The force of an army, for an encore
draws less
Time is but another pesty ton of bricks
Crushing great giants dwelling in mere glory
Flashing in darkness for profits unsought
Steady, Heavy Irish Bailey's brew
The moon gasps for all tonight.

First come the faithful

People will wreck things, they always do

Especially the righteous and true

In the end are the faithful.

1984 – 2001

I'VE HAD MY HEAD BASHED INTO THE WALL
AND NOBODY KNOWS IT
THOUGH I KEEP BASHING EVERYBODY
SO THEY KNOW
I'VE HAD MY HEART TOSSED TO THE WRECKING BALL
AND THROWN MY SOUL TO THE JUNKMAN,

THIS IS WHAT I AM
A FAN OF WHO AM I
WHAT ARE WE, CONTENT?
EVER ENCOMPASSED IN CEMENT
OUT OF TUNE TRIPPING ON HIGH VOLTAGE WIRES
PONDERING MISGIVINGS, TAKING CLUES FROM NON-HIP PIGMIES,
RUNNING OUT OF TIME FOR ANSWERS
SMILING INTO TV SCREENS TO DAZZLE THE NON-SWEARERS
TIMMY'S GOT A TOOTHPICK STICKING IN HIS EYE
                                    INCENSE BURNING
                                    LIFE'S AMUSING
                    DEEP AND STRANGE, NEVER UNVEILED
IT'S ALL PARTA MY
FIFE AND BIRTH, BREATH OF MYSTIC MIRTH

I CAN'T STOP CAN'T DEFEND
THIS EXERCISE NO MORE

I DON'T HAVE A SENCE OF
BEING ALIVE
I FEEL DESIGNED, AFRAID TO LOOK
TOO CLOSELY IN

TO SOMEONE'S EYES

FOR FEAR OF DERAILMENT

INVOLVEMENT IS LOSS OF FREEDOM

I FEEL INSPIRED

BY ECONOMIC NECESSITY
AND IMMORTAL ETERNITY VAST
 A BLACK HOLE

VACUME

SUCKING ME AWAY FROM
LIFE.

F l o y d

Bye- bye braincells, chemtrain a rollin'
talk mace for the bleary eyed,
 Sale at the big one hold musturd trust me take to the beat stall the heat
take a rap kick back shake hands with the big boys
SOUL CHASER MAKIN COOLIE, TOKIN ROVIN MARY
WANNA BAKE A TEPEE?

roll em what your were bred to do, and defend!
It was it was it yes: I can take a tulip to the gig brain
fizzle trickling like candy storms out of the sky, licking
chop children standing
in line for the carnival rides.

It flashed before my eyes,
can we stay
still

      while too late banking on
      gig pig hank man, be stool for the fool, ah shit
Something

      is killing me, tell ya what is is if

youll kindly communicate,
         with me
      heart to heart, head to toe, soul to soul, honestly
I'll be waiting at the door in the rain.

okay crazed reader quickly surveying this program to see if it

arrests your attention and you think, maybe I'll adopt it,

immortalize or toss

it -- this is for you lost lover of fame

and the cosmos getting more

practical sane and boring with every breath looking more like

thirty something,

its your niche

you're no crook

hanging out for gratuity, takin a dive, a

slide on the combine of Custer, the

apple eye face on the bill, man

get a thrill, catch a life, brother my

sympathy goes out to

you who need the news to find meaning and fortune crushed

by descendants of brigadier generals,

ain't it a bummerenlighten it

There's nothing hap'nin at the bar
I know where they are

at the tail end of eternity

d   a   z   z   l   e   d

Soon   summer   be   blowin

copulating creed cream delight

Please Wait

Tea man crest hut sell
dwelling up
nose rod hustle bliss rule death kept control

lude missle fear damned roam free down up hell van

together

circling,

badge fear, a yearning

well warmed mission **love**

bold daring quest closed to pedestrians, cursed
for their lacking praise
their envious happiness
tredding on doing this forever
sending signals from where? to whom?
why am i?

recieving decieved-ieving, grieve for the noose

Squaring off :

                dirt from a bly leaven tank hoe

          outwardwent the lovers

        the angels weren't true

red socks had a run

        and the teddy weren't new.

The Sweat of Misfortune

The sweat of misfortune
remembers misdirection
an alabaster coup
at the edge of
redemption

and then once more
seeking sought diffusion
all that never glittered
was what must have been true

arrived in a box
woo was delivered
the matter now packaged
demerit confused

at loose, an arrangement
caboose to the show
can't stomach the bitter
nor bland adds for news

acknowledging trivia
confronting what? Truth?
no more can be granted
glimpses of the muse

no more time to groove
redemption to prove
against the wall
hammered into

asked to remove
society, win
resolve or lose
never seen again

fever wore the noose
out
at
every jingle blister
race against the clock rush
ing to heavenforevermore
where they wind the yup yup clocks
detriment to deemphasis
can't escape the magnet
generations make molds
and into the factory one goes.

real
life

Ah man it's a tough life
But I'm a gonna pull through
Scrape off the residue
and be
as freshly intune with morning dew
as injuns before booze

Is it, man, a tough life?
I'm asking you,
My mind like a machine keeps grinding out
 clues   Invalid one minute after the next
I'm asking you --
Have you ever arrived
at the belief that you're crazy?
There's always another day coming,
or so we believe

It's a tough life man
I'm doing all I can
to cope with the abstractions
distracting
real
life

Charades

Hello help my long lost love,
 only in your absence it seems
do rockets fuel the dreams

will serenity fill the breeze
greater than today? so stay
away with those realities, so
harsh, so
overbearing, keep
those politics away   I"M

TOO WARPED OUT TO THINK
TO
       START A COASTER ROLLIN
DEAD WRECK ON THE MOTORCADE, BABY GOT IT
          MADE WITH ANOTHER MAN, I GOT
     JUST A SUN
TAN, IN THE SHADE WITH THE
       OLD TIMERS PLAYING
       GAMES OF SHERRADES AND
       LAUGHING,

GrUnGE

Fantastic, telling lies
Pretending music amputates
And love still stimulates

Still in the water

Dreams of innocence lost to

circles round a

stone skipped

It doesn't matter, so just groove

Lest the afternoon be wasted

Popped balloons on the water, floating

Towards rapids of trite death, don't

P a s s   a w a y

I'VE SEVERED THE TIES TO MY OWN FANTASY

AND IF ONLY IT WEREN'T FREE TO DREAM

LIFE WOULD BE A COMEDY AGAIN.

psychedelic resolution

water drops on templates
dissolving blueprints for a new world
setbacks
to short term profiteering smudging tomorrow

matrix music
brain blast
beauty   - . -

calling a look-ahead guru

somewhere afar a go a guitar

stereo feedback attuned to the heart
ner' perfect

for new

f r o n t i e r s .

doomstalling heart a beaut that weren't banned

with radiated sun blisterscarred flesh

it weren't long ago

some amiss merrygoo, had a stall falling

seen as a clue for one good misbeggoten

stored on a nervous heart beating abused

lone on a moonstar, oriental, amused;
silence
grant melody unto we the confused

longing to sail high seas of easy

e c s t a c y ,

modern

e t e r n a l , no backdrop untrue.

they beat their

              guns amok

                          they crowded luck

     dirt fell from their boots,

angels wore brown, their hair cut, briefcased

    as words like matrix conformity

        broke the dew

atomic tests boom and fizzled

     ironic quests fairy taled

                       threw and through

       ice cream cloud clear blue eternity

          i fly through you

i do, I

     do it all for

       the feeling of freedom alive

         wind blows my hair

          and suddenly

               a w a r e n e s s !

The Moon that Hit Me

As we go
beebopping blind down alimo alley, too kind to care
back turned to thelast frontier, behaving on a heavy from taboo
down through the slaughterhole, Up to the moon
backwards bethlehem holds a clue
but what's it we're to do?

Question the fat circus lady, mother superior
Moaning "Help me I need
A fix?"

as the dope buys a new cow mooing
on paid for grass green astro turf and neighbors
aswering martyr call desktops, labeling mixtures
never seizing belief of pissed rangers

     yO, man
my hand ain't out for holding no more. Mind
on a tutor tottler
     who of all of us that ever existed
     knows anything at all
     knows what a big chunk there was to bite off
     sees the dawn Daylight,
at daybreak soon

Sleep

        my whisper free

            the slaves,

            taking on routinewhoa

hip who liveth passed yup afternoon

                  long gutter dead

jail fantasy

      Stopping to roam

      around the universe schoolyard

      , the downtown streets!

      Protesting on the capital lawn

            Falwell to the fantasy

      What's going on?

Go get the cleaners, Santa Claus

is gonna be comin down the chimneysoon, get your sneakers

I smell your organic socks

            Burning up the lawn

Puttit   in whithe world

        a dressing the court of the system

      That nobody knows anything about

            Capital Hill pulled another one out

The news was a thrill

            But who pays he bills?

                              The one thing I learned is that
                                    we as a people
                    Get greedy about our neighbores beady eyed freak
                          and We've lost the neighborhood to our silence.

It comes at you real fast, and there's so much to do

and there's only so much you can do

        (shit, you mean I godda take care a this? Oh shit!)

Check out the dawn

we can build our poetry strong again
                                        p i e in your apple eye
W o r d s y m b o l i c

who cares how fucked up you are
flow with the go
blow with the shmos
and deliquently dine on

borrowed time

like mice racing to and fro.

AmsTeRdAm

drink is death
is melencholy,
agai nst endless folly, falling
down
endless pits
of eternity
down
wondering
where did i go
wrong, whoa
can you feel my deep blue soul?
tell me if you've felt so old
tell me so I know
the jive's no prize
the edge once heaven
now heavens been
struck down
attacked from all sides, fog is numb, dumb
bum get outta my hair. I don't
wanna find you anywhere, can't
hide from the mirror for long, it comes
cracking in the faces of old lovers and foes

as music's hanging

  on a noose beyond

    Amsterdam, so far away

that maybe never will this day

  awake to caress life at bay

the end just another

glossed

over plot, Now what's

that fella?

        say's she wants to ride a streetcar

as far as it goes and get out

in

the rain

falls

dolls break

on the

make I'll take

the idiocy if

it promises

happiness.

Spring Rain Independence

Frontier

There's always some rumble
 of some engine somewhere
 if deep in the distance,

deep in the silence
is where I aim to go
breaking fresh tracks in the snow.

Four Seasons

Many seasons have I passed
Rode the dark horse; stood, my back
 to a white birch, conjuring
magic shadows from troubling dreams
in a fire while autumn
chases summer away,
Blanketing a countryside in gold and red charm --
 an array of recourse for
satellites in the void,

Went this way, that, hung
 around a lot pitching pennies and dimes
Whistling like a new bald head
Until filled pockets, belly and bed
Overshadowed the freshness of morning dew
Threw off to some hustlers my old brown shoe
Wincing a less sincere
 bird call for oily cats in the alley scrapping,

Still fearing
vibrations of anger
speaking through the planet

As eyes of the world watch, anticipating
 more horror than prime time drama
Our hands
 caressing ,
ease these tensions

Our
   m I n d s
 alchemizing beyond
 confusion

our my's become ours

I's turn to eyes and years become real

unfiltered, our hearts
grow
passed anger beyond fear
jealousy and rampant ego pettiness
alienation, we
redemption and seed,
are those beings deciding
quests through eternity,

Been around this world a bit
Whirled and puzzled, put down, propped up
Starved and bloated, bludgeoned, loved
Sideways, unconscious, mistakenly redeemed by random
miracles
    and impenetrable karma
Khakis torn and stained
Blistered skin and wrinkled flesh
Fresh air and outlook, rested, ready
To hop in the saddle and ride
Majestic, ready, full of
pride.

(Many seasons have I passed, cherishing
an ability to recognize
each one leading way to the other).

12.7

Daylight is so short in winter.

You've got to pretend the world isn't cold
and when you're good enough at it
good enough to convince others of it
it won't be

yeah,

The Indiscretion of Solitude

looney tunes on a mattress blinding out jazz
tossed in wrinkled blankets and composed
atop the world whirling freejesus
there's a fresh chill here somehow
I didn't expect to gobble the whole thing down

Crazy crazy crazy crazy
fucking thoughts hot sweaty night can't
sleep

I did remember to feed the pigs
shine the beast and for once
I felt as though I've been discrete
Not blabbing to the world about destiny and compromise
peyton place and twilight ewytes
I've been drinkin' quite a life
I been dancing away my strife
Composing crazy lines and focusing on
the simple beauty of the dawn

waiting
in the indiscretion of solitude
pestered by a desolate longing
to render in tune
the harmonious universe
deeply
incredibly,

Around The Maypole

All this intellectual propensity for love
Abstract credo, a vibrantly

colorful canvass against which all else pales;

As we dance around its maypole wishing
for its hidden heat to reach us

And eventually,
We mistake the dance for the religion
But the beauty is
We're still dancing.

Mingling With Drifts

Once the enticing wind rips
Friends want to be lovers and lovers be friends
Aren't we still all full of love in the end?
Kisses and words and touches and clues
Into the cosmos with a cuddle for the dues
Humans behaving like strange mortals do
Inwardly, awkwardly
  Across the ice and over the edge
Is it
 the heart that sails blindly
   towards the poesy of the wind?
As the soul
  feeling the meaning behind logic so old
Absorbs the snowflakes
while mingling with drifts.

Self

Reclusive, unabrasive, agreeable, raging
dependable idealist romantic spendthrift
impatient distorter of the truth, combustible
unfulfilled, big talker, great hugger,

      Now that my brain is again expanding
      Floating free through time less demanding
      Working up the ambition to rattle
      these aging bones and make muscle,
I see
the afternoon fading
insurmountable.   fresh Earth through my fingers
                      tucking eternity away,
                          grimacing into
pockets of time, smiling
 in the eye of the sun, walking
                in line in a softening hide,   radiated
        by magnificent beams
                    and tides shearing
          independence,

Now that my brain again expands
now that I'm really just a man
now that I smile in the grey afternoon
I fight
 but I falter
between dreams and idle schemes,
beneath full moons and movie screens
a spectator on
  that stage of dawn
 resplendently patrolling aging buds of inspiration, seeking
truth and graciousness, warm breasts, a nest and friendship
sworn to global reckoning and egoless peace gardening
Caught dreaming, dreaming, absent from
these microchips that turn around
economies and consciousness and media fried routines and all
that bullshit that needs wilting,
that grows around and strangles us like
a crushing wild vine ;

I think
    but I waver
Dining with disaster and the mediocrity of being
    Without Vision, Spirit, Hope or Might, nestled
in a cozy slumber wrestling
 with the finest woman, warmest linen, still befuddled
with questions like the gonging clock and nagging rock
n'roll screaming wine and crocus, turnit
up-loud, brainwashed
of hope and high overhead, a low esteem day, freedom
dries like mud in a cup
As another dawn calls on to let dew beads heal
the wounds
of inflicted lobotomy
while
the metronome ticks
 on,

I think
 but I waver
between nature and intent, heaven bent on saving
grace
 to per chance retire
our rapid race
swiftly back to narrows
 spiralling down age old gallows
chained to triteness uttering
 the same old curses, asking
 familiar questions, not
  finding any new answers to help
   set the future into
place,

Far from my apathy I bestow
 an ounce of tenderness to who needs it most
and love comes back heavy like a nagging ball and chain
while I, compelled to crush it, all the ecstacy and pain
reduce again, the world
to cold
 resignation and mediocrity, crying
  naked in the wilderness alone.

Steadfast On The Banks

To walk,
Uncluttered
with bludgeoning thoughts and delirious emotion,
along a path obscured
brilliantly by a blanket
of damp autumn leaves
Early, before the sun
repaints its misty canvas bright,
is to be reborn.

To see beauty in all places
Finding grace within the soot
is
a disposition
that can't be stolen from
or saved,

dancing eloquent on a river flowing swiftly by
these leaves
wave
 farewell,

I stroll in apprehension of the random passing of each life
the sacredness and insignificance
beneath this warm gold awning thinning,

Leaves falling everywhere
Soon the trees will all be bare
Wind swelling while I smile
back
at a myriad of colorswirling

While above me fall remains
 of seasons I hardly knew
slaying critters for the stew.

Transcendence

Sitting in a northern forest
In a pleasant spot, humbled
by towering pines and vibrant red sumac
vast blue sky and easy waters
Whispers the wind of eternity

No answers forming pacts that reek of tyranny
I drift and float
Surmise no gloating, no swift
course of action through the narrows
 of day,

As a soft gleam
From a mysterious realm
precipitates a bewitching

Time and again I feed the itch
moving on in to warm the damp
vibrations of forevermore, lurking
there, just to touch
to reach out
and answer with a smile

for afternoon is only so long as
Whispers the wind of eternity

Blankets

The game changes, or
The aim
of the game

A few years ago
I would've raced off to the mountain
Sneaking frightendly away
      from warmth of the preceding night
Fearful of entanglement

Now,
I really could care less about the mountain
And would rather cuddle under
blankets while the rain
falls outside
forever.

Grateful Jerry

Taking the anecdote, swallowing pride
Mandolin plays a sweet haunting flutter
as life becomes another era,

traveling back
to summer when a night
held so much promise.

Heading on into a tunnel
silent
head bowed, hands folded
Understanding nothing but symphonic ramblings charting
barbaric frustrations awkward in deliverance, attaining some
significance not
real, its not
just a little jimmer jammer, slapping hand jive exchanging
maybes, smiling
in the Mexican sun
Dying
by the limelight of a fire
trying
to get to where life lays
on embarrassments and inner tinglings
dancing visions in the fire, calling up the squires
dying living feeling fine spine extending
heart aching
beautiful
magnificent
epic.

Inside a Forest, Deeply

In the thicket of the morrow
the Grace of day hath rolled away
A gray lock upon the sky,
An everafter lullaby;

I see the hatchet coming down
On an overgroweth Earth
And know a deal going on
Somewhere upon one master's hearth,

Contaminated by a sound
Overhead, from the sky
A wasp looks straight into my eye
I do not quiver, move, nor doubt
the relativity of fear, aggression
as it passes over, leaving
an unscarred
endless sky,

you ask
Was it worth it? Restful?
My response is but a smile
Put on trial.

Asking deep what dreams I sow
What comes to me in deepest hours
How or why, I do not know;

The story goes, familiar
For unknown sorrows do I quiver
Half expanding, the other dying
Do not doubt, my aim is true
I have not hid for fear of you
I have to make peace with the fire
I had to ask my friend, the forest
Amidst such hazards, should I roost?

The forest answers, "My old friend
To see you by yourself again
Brings me to show you fallen bark
And moss upon pebbles once tossed,

When you were younger, and were lost
Seeking shelter from the frost
Could take no remedy or vice
We, The forest provided no wishes
but to lead of life allowing,

As mortal hearts and hands can seldom
Stand and feel such laughter
Indeed, the story goes, and who's to follow?
Resting by a roadside of murderers and lost travellers
Come now to this Earth
for Nothing like the painted frost inside a forest, deeply
Silenced by sounds mysterious, Guided
by an unknown call,

That is not all," the forest cries
"You've hardly seen it with your eyes
You've barely felt, you've seldom known
You cannot live it on your own
You can't abuse this solitude
No deed nor seeds will follow you
dizzying depths of the sky above
The spinning canopy is *love* ."

For here, everafter
For time to call again
I am so humbled in the presence of
my forest, friend
Unaltered, so forgiving
One mustn't cut these old growths down
One mustn't cut the forest down.

The Agony of Emptiness

There's always a party somewhere
If you are fun, you'll find at least one
If you become really alive you'll find there's usually five
or six at any hour close by enough to attend

That's the way I am. Technicolor 3 AM
Laughter too loud, kisses so free
and you got to get going
to the next before your momentum is gone
cause when its
gone
its
  G O N E
baby life
so
empty
staring
up
at
the ceiling of a lonely room
finding
a hole
in the center of my being
that makes my heart ache
and my brain go numb, fearing
a cynic's glare and an old man's crutch
humble
full of aches,

Turning inside is no place to hide,

No peace from within leads no road on to drive. no
substance to lurk upon frontiers with

My heart is heavy
my insides ache
I feel a raw wind blow beneath a cold winter's moon
and fear I'm perfectly in tune
with the agony of emptiness.

Cosmic Groove

Easy music
I wanna make
easy music
that makes stern people smile
and entertains passersby
for a while
and maybe afterwards they'll retain
a little piece of heaven
I've uncovered,

E a s y   M u s i c ,

All I wanna do is lay down my song
sense the dew and roll in the dawn
Brain fried, lobotomized, I'm
all through hobbling with conventional combatants --
        aerosol and petrohaul and factual derangements
Stir the stew, ain't nothing new
feet cemented from the lawn
queuing up for cobwebbed ruins, I'm through
aspiring to fools' deeds at the roost,

> *It's all karma*
> *if you're not getting love*
> *you're not giving,*

E a s y   M u s i c ,
All I wanna do is garden and swim
at ease with a current that won't drowned a friend
watch seasons change, dig their attributes while sustaining
creatures turning off
to yesterday's outrageous love
and to their own
commiserating 'neath rainsoaked cardboard, shivering,

Easy music
                    I wanna make
        easy music
that lives on the sweet breeze
and dances in trees

all

I wanna do

is sing

true to you, feeling
your tender touch, basking in your glow
as silent everafters unfold
symphonically majestic, simple and Cosmic
as the interplay inside a spider's delicate
web,
easy
music I wanna make
easy music, not
extend curses or magnifying ruin, but
                                    just get on

transcending weary destiny
 inner enemies and doomed routines
                                    Transcend!

Feeding natures needs
from nature's seeds,

beeping
  heartbeat
whispering
  concrete
      tell me
answers, no despair
send a shiver
across my flesh, lets share
our hidden understanding of glorious possibilities
everywhere, seems we've

succumbed too much, accepting
sickness as convention, does the essence of our souls know
    what commodity
weighs our hearts?

Out of tune with intuitive logic buried in a box of ivory tower
journals
I know it all can't be
easy music
Cause there's madness that keeps leaking out of my head
Things I should normally never have said
as I wander
heavier than air, trying to catch
the breeze, wondering
who knows or holds answers or a clue to unknot
 understanding of all of this
questionably relevant
cosmical stuff?

accordion rollercoaster

I thought
I'll buy you a mandolin
and learn to play it with you
trading licks and harmonizing
until our notes are one
Strong
soulful
erotic
loving,

but the rollercoaster will jerk and twist
and I know it won't all be
easy music
depths come from the highs and lows
drama on the brow, sorrow in the fall

as truth continues to dwell
 outside
our firm duet.

Sunrise Trail, February

Feeling dizzy under the stars,

Fading away, those stars and I
Clouds are coming between us,

A chilly wind, hisses
Through the dark and giant pines
so small am I
as the wind erases my tracks in the snow,

Still dreaming of paradise
utopian eden, love and peace
Still feeling a need to place a stone
moving silent
 through the forest wild
 without having made
a home.

Relativity

Time slides away, we all know
 throwing our best pitches into the wind
Scarcely noticing
mysterious storm clouds
fast approaching
from within,

Each with our own centered universe, Engrossing
all that is reachable
Enjoying a multitude of dimension
Now and forever, a rain-
drop
on tall waves of
an ocean vast.

The Sum of Destiny

Some make money, Some make love
Some make trouble
Some make all of the above
Some make peace, some make charms
some make art, some make arms,

Sometimes I cast my eye upon the sun
And wonder if there's any bit of insight I've won
By teetering on total freedom
Somewhere between leisure and nothingness
As a lazy, not so abstract cove
Calls out to melt the ice and snow,

Sitting in the morning sunrise
Contemplating all that may arise
Unfettered with cares and watered down woes
Or tremors of boisterous, unfaithful odes,
Driven to the brink of a new reconciliation
Aloof to the aims of that old soliloquy
Afternoon twists, and moves on an arrangement
Never quite sure if its you
or its me,

Climbing to see, aching in woe
Destiny once again takes its toll
Is it easy to know? It's painful to feel
All of the entertainments n'er real
Going for broke, there's no other way
No one can stop the sneer of dismay
No soft rocks or jagged flowers
Perch on the edge of untraveled hours,

So it happened to you, It happens to me
Sometimes so blinding I cannot see
The weight of the soul grows akin with the heart
Twisting and seeking to just play a part
in this grand
       symphony on the highway of love,
            Over and under
   Majesty and doubt
I've heard it before, I feel it again
Life carries on like a swaggering gem
Taken away, awakened from death
No scene magnifies like being tossed over the edge
Into the depths, in tune with
All chaos, circling, beautifully
The drama of the universe.

tea

It used to make sense
All this late night jibberish
stretching the brain around a little
justifying all the scruffy righteousness, it all
made so
much sense

back then
when
days were dynamo, but these
are glory nights, loving
frightfully on the edge
like real lovers do
nothing near
as fresh, yet
can't get passed
or drive out
those ambassadors of relevance
sideways on another track
carnivores of upward bent
pickers and complainers
knee surgery retainers
alibis so interesting
who cares about the truth?
Soldered on a backlot dog, wandering
fro and too
eloquent
innocent
cyberdom
filibuster
nonsense
at the backdoor fence
frivolous and free
on a teacup, whispering
silent
loving
crisp.

L.

Love is nervous Jerry Lewisness

tossing, turning, unable to

sleep

misery

superhuman feats

walking on air

sincere breakfast

New by golly, just
thinkin'
about taking a roller coaster ride
somewhere
over the rainbow
down like a tepee
afar from teevee

All these crazy
people doing
all this crazy shit
outta time
outta rhyme
somehow on mars, alley-
oop bars guitars neon stars, we are
gone
baby gone go
roam
your
home
work's in the oven burning, I
love you I
do
I
do it
all for the love of
you.

gettin' sleepy
wanna dance
to an italian accordion
catching
 the chill of the night air
over
a bottle of red wine
with you.

Beluga Slough

Will anyone understand
These colors and this subtle motion
  beckoning art to a standstill?

No angle wide or deep enough to
capture this sensation of eternity

or if the technology does exist
It's too much apparatus, its weight
would crumble
the delicacy
of rocks and grasses

Eyes closing to dreams of multicolored
birdlike creatures cawing, unafraid
of human warnings
marvelous and mean.

why I quit going to the movies

I see your smile
superimposed
over each frame of the movie
over each landscape
your brown eyes
deeply falling into mine
I wanna stop time
and make love to you for
two thousand years.

Beside the Nuke Plant

Another day, another holler
Another groove worn in tomorrow
Tucking rare late-season flowers in our collars
 questioning
 the whole grand workings of it all
Held in place by an arrogant glue
Toxic, unbreakable

Where lover's embrace in a ridiculed meadow
Arriving late yet caressing
a future built
upon a tranquility to come
unjaded by the mocking crows
Guarded secure by steadfast pines
 outlining the sky,

All pretense loosens, history stops
 for a precious drop
of dew upon
an everipe meadow.

thank you

The hurricane that is my life
Circles round me dizzy like a deadpan artifact of
some crazy matinee

epitomizing
Youth

but where did the metamorphosis go?
Sideways towards a hankering
of forgiveness for trite
echoes of a golden slumber, an awkward
life of promises, n'er
connecting

n'er
knowing
where to go, when
to act upon the soliloquy or dive
sunglasses on, down
sworn to fashion and daily fads
far out from the spectrum, barely
hanging on

What are these moments of our lives
Measured out
in side by side reasoning?

It's all what's in your mind, my brain
is on fire, rendering
waves and fireworks impossible
to grasp, flying
high over the everyday
tasks of living, immune
to biology, hustling
for a firetruck
screaming
at silent flames of blue,

the hur-
icane of our
chaotic lives, swirls-

We're talking here, of the tempest
 all around, haphazard and hairy
under and over, backwards and sideways,
limbs stretching hands touching breasts feeding muscle leading
forward towards the glorification of
trumpets sounding, blowing
loud vacancies away, fantastic
sunrise yawning with a grin
huge and overwhelming
impossible to hide
a neverending memory
built in heater for the rain,
thank you.

Spring Rain Independence

Spring bubbling up through the ice
Sending icebergs sailing south
Waterfalls begin to drip
Soon to gush with effererent grace,

Is there something really in the air
When the bold forget their independence?
When country begs to be explored
    Ambition wanes to be ignored
  Is springtime more
            than nonsense?

Moist the soil, damp the rain
The brightest sun lukewarm and tame
  Thunder rolls away,

Laughter in the afternoon
No thoughts at all of night or snow
There's springtime in the face of us
Who've come to smile, and come to swoon,

If something's not made of this moment
It's bound to fade away
Day's prime is not worth limiting
Sunlight flickers off your waves
Your breasts so lovely, unconcealed
Squinting, I feel air of spring,

Grant room to make this wonder last
Amidst old thoughts of wasted bliss
I've sight as far as sight need be
Enchanted by a sign of spring,

Breasts so sweet on which I sleep,
The world's pillow precious
Dies beneath steadfast stone pillars
Marking progress, but what for?

The pleasures we adore don't
Change much all through history
Close your eyes and feel the breeze
In time we'll turn gold like the leaves
For now our grin is foolish, birds are birds
We needn't waste time up with words.

Absurdity

Even if the prize can't be won
Love drives the stride on
Foolish carrot in front of the hare
Gets that bunny around,

Spreading those seeds about
Love's intoxication
        the most contagious of all strengths
Conjures up a communal warmth,

Don't look away
Though it'll surely hurt
No richer nugget sparkles
 up death's shadows.

Excellent

You've got a private
smile that blossoms like a flower
When I say, *I love you*

dipping in the moonlight
Your body, mine
naked and wet
Our skin
sensitive
our hearts
beating
gasping for breath
Exhilarated
truly
alive

Warmth Measured

A warm blanket

A warm body

A warm bed

A warm home

What other necessities

Could invalidate these luxuries?

Oh Woe

What strange satori is this?
Bewitched, beheaded
I ache
With all the indemnifying ridicule of ages
Sleepless and weary and facing insignificance
Not free, heart heavy, focused only
on a glimpse of possibility
Impossible leap, destined fall
Yet no other jewel seems to shine much at all
No air smells as sweet
No other aim worthwhile, no other peace
Oh woe
is me
Oh woe.

Confession

Magistrate, of late
I've been too preoccupied by Love
Dreams of it, lack of it
Smothered by it, doubting
Whether I can pull it off as sweetly
as I can imagine it,
Compromise is a delicate art
and Life such a short, sweet snuggle
All mixed up with toil and trouble
Substance to sustain the soul
Sometimes I feel so old and worn
Too many memories
For anything new to compete with
Cynical, weary
Seems I'll never fall in love again
When at the same time
I'm always in love, with everyone
Everywhere
I've a hankering to give birth
to something special for the earth
No madman's riddle or lover's plea
But something true, that will always be.

January

What you share is what you share
faucets of erotic madness
under
blankets warm against winter's
frozen
ice
reflecting
the cold moon
shivering
with petrified
dimension
humbled
in the gobbling of
air.

Agnes

1.

When I couldn't speak to you I
couldn't stop
thinking about you I
had to write these words
to validate my passion
to give credence to all the sleepless nights
I had to ask for you in my dreams
 and rub visions of you out of my head at daylight
I had to medicate the pain and run insane to outpace
 my heart grown weary by your smile
your scent, keen sense and
loving eyes
my demise
upsidedown spun weary sickening
heaving grand opportunities up
for what I really hope is love
coming around
up the back
silent
unsure
in denial
trying to forget
losing sleep
going insane
dig the rain
agnes
who I love too much to leap out at with my own impatient goals
whom I love too much to kiss
to bring you into my absurd poetic universe
that teeters always on insanity
that should be sane
that should be intertwined with you, but
damn do I
want you always to be fine

forever and ever
I don't want me to fuck you up
I love you too much
and it isn't healthy for one to be soo
in love
obsessed
absent minded
immune
to logic and practicalities
responsibilities and loyalties
all I want
is you
all I think about
 is you
every hour, every day
I think of you, your ways
the way you hand the bums a dime
and take in stray dogs
and sort the bills
and tell me how a woman thinks, I think
I love you, madly
I really do
and even though its really
fucking me up, still I think
that I should be
with you
so
let me make my once more ode
and try to hold my breath
again.

2.

So many scattered edges
The higher you climb, the farther you fall
So many things promised, Too Much
Need to focus, settle down
Life is really simple

(All that really matters to me is
water, trees and community
fresh air to breathe
integrity
some food to eat
and love
good, sweet love
enough to keep the world grooving
On without any harm
-ful dawns or discarded beer cans in the creek
We don't need that
There's already gonna be enough bleeding
just being alive Causes bleeding)

On the outside looking in
Awkwardness with a gracious grin
Simplicity, weightless being
Except for the gravity of soul

Trappings of an old dogs tricks
Habits hard to lose or fix
Acceptance of imperfect hues
Invitation to lose or higher truth?

Don't know how I'm gonna keep it all together and make sweet
love to you
But it's life
What finer thing is there to do?
When all is so rugged and pure and vast
These purple and pink flowers on the side of the highway bring
me back to you
Girl you,
Your touch your eyes your smell
Your warmth, your splendor
Your whole demeanor
Cuddling me tight,

Is it you I'm driving to the top of the world to forget
or to see if you're still in my brain when I reach the top of the
world?
Then I'll know I'm insane because love is insane
And life is insane cause most were born out of love,
No logical rhyming reason, season or science to it all
It's just the way things move, harmony on the breeze
Disharmony at sea
It can't be proved
There should be music
here
and everywhere
music
from our souls feeling the world
fueling our souls
feeding our world
Do animals hear music?
Does a field mouse make music?
Does a caribou like to dance?

Well beyond the means of youth's grand
 promise and bewitching gleam
Still swimming the magnificent stream
Dreaming, smiling, breathing
Making time and bridging scenes
A sense of truth less often
Rears its head to lose the coffin
Suffered and geared for, stripped away
of dismayed rhymes of reason
until there's nothing left but skin and bones
and the gravity of soul.

Down on the farm I dreamed of Paris
And there in the Opera House made good whoopie
How can each new kiss compete
With all those adolescent feats?
Falling into your bright eyes makes me feel so old
Aching with the gravity of soul.

How am I gonna keep it all together and make sweet love to you?
Too many worlds to balance, reckless urges and insanity
Mixed with fine elegance
style and passion, we've got
          P a s s I o n !
Rest your head in mine and trust me, I've got
nothing
to hide from you, I'll
confess my every thought, every dream
if you will help me be with you
making sweet love, keeping the universe
together
harmoniously
in tune.

3.

Broke the ice
Shouldn't have
But I couldn't help myself
Nature, in its organic uncontrollable majesty called
And I had to crawl
Beyond the frost

I done what I did
And there ain't no undoing
You can hold your breath only so long
enough to just dive in, then back
to the surface, gasping
splashing

Thanks for the heartache, Sorry about the mess
Troubled hearts, troubled minds
Going for the forbidden zone
Going to what matters,

I had to take time out
I had to be a fool in love
To seek nothing but
The infinity in a lover's eye

Love is absolute folly
Nourishing
Supreme intoxication
Potent, rendering useless
Rational pursuits of honor
    with a thorny brush and a wince,

I did what I did and there ain't no undoing
Thanks for the heartbreak, sorry about the mess
I did all that I could to put myself last
Letting others live and die in the spotlight
until I couldn't hold back anymore and had to strut my stride
Had to
Break the ice
Had to be true

Because I wanted you to know
For sure
As if my antics weren't enough
My serenades and foolish grace
Apologies and invitations
Gifts and gracious toasts,
another chess game soon began
Not afraid to win or lose, I move
Forward, irregardless,

>   Is it possible that love is so blind
>   That we never shared in all this time?
>   Have you not any of these tough and warm
>   memories to recollect?

Thanks for the heartache, sorry about the mess
I thought you were a cut above the rest, something special
Irresistible and divine
For all these years that I've had you on my mind
I could die today just knowing you
But I want you to know, my life is true
And I would live it all
for you

Sorry about the mess
Following the heart seems to widen the soul
And soul is what we call our own
Standing after the deluge still
shaking off the flurries of another winter's chill,

Still look pretty good, I got color in my face
Hope that I can go out with grace,
Making it on a few more dawns
Before passing the hat to cooler Jacks,

Hid behind the promise of a strange surprise
I never seen a bad sunrise
I've never feared the consequence
of living for today
discounting dismay in favor of
the infinite possibilities of love,

Close your eyes and what do you feel?

Listening to the wind howl
and the world moan

sighing
in the ecstacy of warmness.

The Gravity of Soul

dawgonnit
thought I had a clue but no
twas only a desert mirage
strike up the band, back to the party
I wasn't going anywhere
anyway
nah

I wasn't
really
grooving on those
sensations of
yours
all
that
much
any
way.

Communicating at an Unknown Rate

It's cold outside
the rain is falling, frozen
ice chunks
tapping
on the window, the walls
are shivering
the fire's out
Yet still I'm here with you again
Listening to the silence
Dreaming of connection
Searching for redemption
Harboring temptation
Love is so divine
So dignified
So warm and tight,

What're we telling each other with our unspoken words?
What're we living and dying for?
Why are we together? Why are we apart?
This distance is breaking my heart
No medicine or remedy
No greater cohesion to contrast
This be all, my love
Let us bicker, sweat and bathe
Together in our own cosmic
 Quest and communion
Righteously aghast
with a truth too succulent
to comprehend.

The Sting

Time Zapped
 Out of existence forever
 can't get
enough don't
butter them pastries, I got
too much on my side for pride
Don't wanna ride when I can walk
True and unbitten
  by blisters of love and conventional wisdom,
A weird fella, I know
  that's why my home is a rolling stone.

That's why misfortune balks at the beggars
Teetering vibrations that hurt like a leaper
Drowned in an atmosphere of divine intervention
Let out on a stage to be redeemed,

Scary plot, Unlawful twist
Why don't I just slit my wrist?
Heaven found underground
No need hustling for home cooked fish
Nobodies comin' round this time
You, me, Anyone, We're
All retired,
Be in
front of the teevee or out back by the crick
Bring the old man's walking stick
Toke the gravy and spice the rye
You got a bug up in your lazy sty
Buzzing, flapping
Hard to focus on
That I bet.

50%

The enemy is within
trapped
inside a jungle full of misconstrued autopsies
Saving grace, remodelling
the waste
that cannot be erased

faced and found
knowledge driven
by a jarring revelation
by the way,
the railroad bed
so tough and full of blood is
the decapitated soul of the native

this realization feasts

on destined treaties
grace and virtue
A dream of tomorrow we used to
wake to

ah,
suck up the marrow of stupidity
what nobler foolishness than love
warms the heart
of our karmic songs,

sun fading 'neath the skelital
hibernating trees
I have no such luxury as these

must stay up and brave the winter to walk through waist deep
        snow

sometimes I get to thinking about outer space
wondering about the human race
laughing at the columbine plowing the field
eager to harvest, anxious to yield

seems like old times we've grown accustomed to
me and you
drifting
apart
lifting
the veil
of our shrouded insincerity
and cosmic inability
to transcend
our traps
those things in the mirror that we call self
twisted realities and beautiful reasons
  didn't we have seasons?
Like the snow, like spring
tarnished visions

fading

fading

spring rain

it's beautiful
  hear
  the rain, smell the rain, feel
  cold chills pushed in through
the open windows by
  the rain,
        yeah
  heaven
    by flickering
  candle-
  light silent
      only
  the sound of rain

    dripping

Noon

What, really, does it matter
that I didn't get done those things
 that seemed so important yesterday?
Only today's
awkward weight
of insignificance lurks
upon my alien brain
sheltered by the fresh sunshine
of another ripening day.

I'll be no good, racing
from daybreak to dusk
chasing
utopian riddles
an imprisoning conquest, remaining
forever a fool,

Lying in tall grassy fields of eden
Beyond the revolution, daydreaming
about spring flowers as
nightmares of war and industrialization
are but ashes settling in the earth,
flickering like a shadow of history in my vision,

The air so fresh and choice
Today
comfort
to rest just in the sun
ambitionless
alive
immune
to the distractions of a pig.

happenings

somewhere on a Sailing Ship
racing atop Waves
The perfect lover, perfect
friend doesn't
exist
but
there's plenty to get by on
sweeping new lovers off of their feet
guffawing with all the fine characters to meet
there's plenty to get high about
rattling cages of discontent open
out to the sun-
shine glorious

Taking
a
trip
along any
route
is a gas
getting kicks
with screaming tribesman
adventure edging
 living another
day
on
Happenings.

Regrets

Regrets? I wish
I'd spent more time loving
Less time drinking
Less time trying to understand the lost
And more time cultivating the inspired

My old clothes
are dark and worn
And heavy, I'd like
To leave this hairy duffel behind
walk naked through a fresh shower
To robe again in light, bright colors
To feel the eternity of mothers
Dining on health and knowing that wealth
Has nothing to do with material salvation
Or status, false notions or grimacing gains
or compromised strains of cohesion bought
at a liquor store out by the tracks,

Wishing I took more pictures
Instead of just hangin' out
Capturing life, For what, I'm not sure
Maybe to weigh when the living is done
I'd like to breathe some more in the sun
I'm not yet really done being young
When we be men we be
strong, proud and dumb, Eager
to let women take us on
So we curse as we drink
We will die like the lotus
After rising like yeast
Regrets? I wish
The grass wasn't always greener
Somewhere else
And I could just be more
Comfortable with myself.

Then and Now

We had some good times
remarkable, erotic
Now the war is over.

I feel like reaching out
to touch you but I haven't got
a clue as to
Where
this bold and weary world has left you
tonight,

the time has soared, the threads're split
a meal is roasting on the spit
and I'm not sure
if I've dug my proper grave
or if satin calls the knave,

It's hard to know, It's hurts to feel
and no one knows concealed fear
I'm keeping pace with the motions alright
while growing more alien to my inner light,

I was so much younger then
come full circle now, I'm
up to the challenge you presented then
but haven't a clue as to where you're found.

Souvenirs

Fire beginning before the sun goes down
before darkness
falls eloquent
silent
atop a tyranny of daytime, subtly retreating
unto a found significance, lazing
idle by its flames,

Neither here nor there
Looking beyond a glare, a sneer
Hurled in the direction of the damnedest
Fury beheld, vibrant
 Full of
smiles
from pain
wrinkles
from sun
Eyes that have seen
Hands that have touched, blistered, bled, caressed

Neither
here nor there, Uncentered
Insignificant
Towering
Head and belly growling
Alone, Roaring
Through another forest
roaming
Collecting stones and souvenirs
and songs
To entertain the throngs
Of folks in every port, at every fire
Smiling and alive
Heartful, none deprived
as tenderly, affection
Sizzles
forevermore
as but another passing memory
of life upon the road.

Walk On

Where my heart calls its home
Is a misty morning road away
From whatever magic fills the night,
Whatever blight lives on the vine
Leads on again towards
Another shore less foreign,

As some are lucky
in love and comfort
Others get rich
In strange adventure,

And it all probably leads to the same
Weighing of loneliness and love
Flowers always brighter on the other side of the stream
Seems its cold current
Gets tougher to cross with each rising tide
as we accept
Who we are and who we aren't
What we have and have not
Resigning
to mortality's grazing
of grasses and clouds.

Winter Blues

Yo Rainman,
Heavy sky been reigning
  for some months now, wish it'd end
I'm rocking in an old man's chair awaiting spring
Awaiting to be born again
Hoping spring brings
rejuvenation, sun drenched afternoon
      intoxication, don't think I got no
love left inside my soul
ain't a wink of cheer
that don't seem false
Caffeine only gets me wired and nervous
Booze shoots too quick into a hungover abyss
and psychedelics make
the world too bizarre to fake,
Music all sounds old, I'm rocking
in silence watching
wind coercing trees
as near frozen rain taps desperate before sliding
 poetic down the rattling pane
and Rainman,
What bugs me most is so many seem ailing
and I'm too lame to do a thing about it
You can't spread peace if it ain't in your soul
of cobwebbed confusion, Burst from the sky
you're grand bow Yo Rainman
Make lightning scold, Roll the sky fierce!
Bury deep with your thunder the end of this winter
the Earth is in wait, to bloom fresh anew
 all creatures are eager to serenade the spring dew
These empty vines need some sun to absorb
Cabin fever is driving us mortals near mad
Please,
Open your door to the sky, yo Rainman
Open your gates to the sun.

Mayday

Gather children
can't you feel
fresh drops
of heaven falling
splashing,
Waking us to grow
out of the ground to dance
cosmically true
and in tune
together
in our gracious
garden among
the universe

All the peoples of the Earth
All the animals and birds
Every tree and flower precious
All life a unique entity
Together meshed in harmony

Gathering to thaw
frostbitten morals, misguided on ice
unseeded puddles,
love is the lord
gathering together,
our souls stored
shared

the reward is the wear.

Come together
Come in tune
Love each other
There is room
To breathe
and grow
commune and seek
fail and folly
again
and again

Dancing children
can you feel
fresh drops
of heaven
falling?

Fifty-five Oaks

I forgot how sweet the Earth could be
Sternly soaked by a brisk spring rain

Ancient Oak splashed and watered
Grandfather Entity!
living exclamation, catching

big fresh drops falling

reawakened

into the trivialness of my destiny
by the deep abyss of the apocalypse.

Index of Titles, First Lines and Original Book Sources

Poem titles appears in *italics*. Books in which the poems originally appeared are abbreviated as follows:

EE	Effervescent Ecstasy
AITC	Aloof Inside The Cockpit Searching for the Promised Land
MM	The Modern Mountain
FITS	Fleas Inside The Store
SFTGG	Soulfood to GoGo
NINFCB	Nature is Not For Cardboard Boxes
ABFTF	A Buskin For The Frump
G	GrUnGe
SRI	Spring Rain Independence